Active Parent Concern

Active Parent Concern

A New Home Guide to Help Your Child Do Better in School

Terrel H. Bell, M.D.

GROSSET & DUNLAP
A FILMWAYS COMPANY
Publishers • New York

To Betty Ruth who provides an inspirational example
of Active Parent Concern for our four sons,
Mark, Warren, Glenn, and Peter.

Copyright © 1976 by Dr. Terrel H. Bell
All rights reserved
Published simultaneously in Canada
Library of Congress catalog card number: 76-47997
ISBN: 0-448-16804-9
First Grosset & Dunlap edition 1979
Printed in the United States of America
Published by arrangement with Prentice-Hall, Inc.

PREFACE

This book is dedicated to what I consider to be a neglected but essential factor in the equation for success in childhood learning. Stated quite simply, the prime ingredient is *active parent concern*. Parents are the child's first teachers and the home is the first classroom. In many ways parents are the most influential teachers in the child's life. They can either greatly enhance or actually obstruct learning.

In carrying out my responsibilities as United States Commissioner of Education, I had the opportunity to study the characteristics of unusually successful schools all over the nation. I soon learned that the best schools are located in neighborhoods where parents are actively involved in the learning activities of their children and where the schools are constantly reaching out to encourage parent participation. Indeed, during my years as a teacher, university professor, superintendent of schools, and chief state school officer this belief in active parent stimulation of learning in the home has been strengthened.

PREFACE

In recent years there has been a tendency on the part of many parents to assume that all of the teaching responsibilities for their children will be effectively taken over by the schools and day-care centers. My experience over a long period of time leads me to conclude that this is an assumption that is leading to less than adequate education for our nation's children. As a parent, you should assume some of the responsibility for your child's learning opportunities. But you should be encouraged by the fact that your teaching responsibilities can be carried out somewhat casually as you work, live, and play with your child in the natural setting of your home and neighborhood. I do not imply that this responsibility is an easy one, but it is not a monumental task nor will it take unreasonable portions of your free time. As you read this book, you will learn that it can become a most enjoyable experience for you as you build a new pedagogical relationship with your children.

The finest heritage parents can give to their children is a good education. And to bestow this gift, parents must first of all give of themselves. By applying a few simple techniques described in this book, parents can stimulate their children to reach remarkable levels of intellectual achievement. They can bring to full fruition the innate talents and latent capacities of their children.

Through the years I have tried to determine the many factors that contribute to excellence in learning. I have concluded that no school can fully compensate for failure in the home. Parents provide the stimulation and create the climate for a positive self-image in their children. This is done through a trusting, caring, and sharing relationship that grows out of active concern on the part of parents that every day in the child's life be a challenging learning experience. This comes through incidental teaching that flows from continuous events in the child's life when interest is high and new ideas are born.

From your study of this book you should master a technique that is known as *incidental teaching*. Through faithful application, this new skill will help you to help your child develop a more powerful intellect.

It is hoped that this book will lead you to the great pleasure and fulfillment of nurturing new heights of enlightenment and unexcelled levels of intellectual growth for your children.

T.H.B.

Contents

	Preface	v
	Introduction	ix
Chapter 1	Family Life and Learning: How to Nurture Positive Attitudes in Children	1
Chapter 2	Motivation and Self Image: The Keys to Success in School	21
Chapter 3	The Home Based Curriculum and the Incidental Teaching Method	35
Chapter 4	What You Should Know About Your Child's School	59
Chapter 5	Understanding and Supplementing the School Curriculum	73
Chapter 6	What You Should Know About School Tests and Examinations	101
Chapter 7	Counseling and Guiding Students at Home and at School	123
Chapter 8	What to Do When Your Child Is Failing in School	139
Chapter 9	A Final Message	153
Appendices		161
Appendix A	The School and the School System Bureaucracy	163
Appendix B	Parents, PTA's and School Boards	176
Appendix C	Recommended Reading	186
	Index	189

INTRODUCTION

Education is a cooperative endeavor which involves the student, the teacher, the school, the home, the community, the school district, and the state government. Nothing can compensate for parents' failure to inculcate a desire for education in the home environment and for their refusal to support the learning process. This support must be continuous. It must be manifested in both the attitudes and the actions of parents all through a child's public school years.

This is not to say that parents are more important than teachers in educating children, for both are indispensable to success. There have been many instances in which students have been successful in school and in later life despite having been raised in extremely disadvantaged circumstances or by negligent or incompetent parents. Moreover, some students succeed in spite of having poor teachers. But these are exceptions and are indeed rare. *Most instances of unusual educational accomplishment are accompanied by active, supportive, education-minded parents.*

INTRODUCTION

Education takes teamwork between the school and the home. Not everything is taught at school; nor does all of the learning take place at home. Learning is an ongoing process that continues from birth to death. All human experience teaches something—for good or ill.

Parents have the greatest impact upon the lives of children. Successful children are usually the products of the efforts of dedicated parents. The public school system provides the formal instruction where the fundamentals of reading, mathematics, language, social studies, science, the arts and humanities, and career education and career skills are taught. But bolstering this formal instruction are usually parents who have been active each day in giving the encouragement necessary for their children to show outstanding educational accomplishment. They must care enough to spend the time needed to encourage the very best efforts from their children.

If a child is to gain the most in developing all of his or her latent talents, the child must receive daily support, psychological reinforcement, and recognition in the home environment. In today's education this requires knowledgeable parents who are actively sponsoring an educationally supportive home where learning is part of living and living *is* learning.

Experienced parents know that children are often unwilling learners and that they frequently rebel against instruction and direction from parents. That is why the incidental approach to parental instruction is emphasized in this book. From your reading you should learn to think and act as a friendly and sympathetic teacher as well as a parent. And as you play this new role you will soon find that your child's learning will grow out of incidents that are natural, ready-made teaching opportunities. Through this approach you will be able to overcome a substantial part of the resistance and rebellion found so often in parent-child relationships. Your role as teacher will be interwoven as an integral part of your lifestyle with your child.

In learning to apply the incidental teaching technique, you should be aware of the school, its teaching program and curriculum, and how your child's formal learning can be enriched and enhanced by your casual teaching in the home. Through the interaction of your thoughts as you read the ideas contained in this book, you will learn about schools, teachers, school administrators, the formal school curriculum, educational tests and measurements. You will learn how to help your child as he or she encounters problems at school. It is hoped that this knowledge will help you to recognize and overcome small problems at school before they grow into enormous difficulties.

Without sweeping aside the plain fact that your responsibilities as a parent are quite heavy (and the road is not always a smooth one), through this book you should gain the confidence that you can become a very effective and influential parent-teacher as you apply the basic ideas presented.

Recent studies of student achievement and failure in school indicate that active parent concern and involvement in the child's educational endeavors are extremely crucial factors in determining the degree of success experienced by the child. Student achievement seems to be high in homes where parents talk about education and keep the child constantly aware that education is of the utmost priority in the minds of the parents. Where the conversation seldom centers on school affairs and the educational life of the child, impressions in the minds of young learners are that schoolwork in not essential. Recognition of good work done at school, encouragement to master difficult subjects, parental attention to school activities, and enlightened discussion of report cards are all indicators of a parent and child team solidly committed to excellence in learning.

This book is intended to serve as a parents' guide to education—not only to formal education as sponsored by the schools, but informal and incidental education as sponsored by the home, the neighborhood, the church, and the community. The reader will learn how to help the child learn. This parents' guide should serve as a handbook and reference manual to assist parents in promoting the greatest educational opportunities and highest educational standards at home and at school. *It is intended to motivate parents to supply the very best in home support of the school and to provide an incentive for the school to support the efforts in the home. But more importantly, it is intended to promote the educational, social, emotional, and attitudinal development of the child by helping parents be effective teachers, counselors, and advocates of education for all youngsters from kindergarten through high school.*

1.
Family Life and Learning: How to Nurture Positive Attitudes in Children

In this chapter you will read about the *ideal* situation in the home, the atmosphere that ideally supports and motivates learning. We will discuss the ten characteristics of a family with high potential for nurturing learning and for building the very best in interpersonal relationships. We will then describe the ultimate in human personality development as we encourage you to be concerned about the influence of your home upon the personalities of your children. The discussion will then move to how your home tends to mold character and shape the total personalities of your children. In all of this, in order to advocate the best, we will describe the *ideal* circumstances.

Needless to say, few of us reach all these optimum standards of performance and behavior in our homes. The realization that your own home does not do so should come as no surprise to you nor should it be a source of discouragement. In most families there are some strengths, some weaknesses, and some problems that can easily be solved with a little extra effort. None of us solves all our family problems, nor do we have peace, harmony, tranquility, and the highest of motivation and encouragement every day for our children. The fact that you are reading this book indicates that you are likely to be interested in making progress toward higher levels of family living which will build those positive attitudes and shape those desired attributes of character and personality that your children deserve. This chapter should lend encouragement to you in this direction.

How can one become an effective, active, concerned parent? The beginning is simple. Any parent can start by being an exemplary model. You can make an enormous contribution to your child's success and happiness by just being a good model to follow, teaching first by the example of your own life.

"What you're doing is ringing so loud in my ears that I can't hear what you're saying." This time-worn expression is used in many circumstances. Yet it is an appropriate beginning for a parents' guide to educating the school age child, for we teach much more by example than we do by admonishing or even by expounding precepts to our children. Children first learn by imitating the actions of others, long before they learn by rote.

As you think about being a good living example to your children, it is important to keep in mind that this does not mean that we should strive to hide our human faults from our children. Most parents who love their children and give them normal care and attention are good models for children. But we should remember that we do teach by example as much as we do by our words. The main point is that we should avoid acts of unwitting hypocrisy, because our lives should sincerely support what we want our children to be.

CREATING A LEARNING ATMOSPHERE

Learning in the public schools must be supplemented and enriched by the activities of parents in the home. The home should provide motivation and it should constantly uplift the child not only intellectually but morally and spiritually. Only with roots implanted in a home environment that is oriented to education will the child be nurtured to achieve the utmost in education.

Parents should demonstrate commitment to education by establishing a home in which learning is emphasized. Books, magazines, and reading materials should surround the child during the growing years. A quiet place for him or her to study and constant parental encouragement and support of intellectual activity should be provided.

Children should be aided in learning to read and study early in their lifetime. Since a good beginning counts in great measure toward ultimate success, parents should organize their home and family routine into a learning environment where hunger or thirst for knowledge is as important as for food and drink. Thus the child will accept as a natural part of life the need to study in order to add to the knowledge already gained—if the parents will provide both the proper atmosphere and the daily routine. Reading, studying, and learning should be a natural part of the home routine. The child should grow up feeling that learning is a way of life and a normal part of living.

Most humans persist in repeating actions that were learned early in life, especially if such activities were pleasurable and rewarding. By providing pleasant surroundings for reading and study and by making the study experience agreeable and rewarding, the parents take a significant step in building true support for education at home. *Help your child grow up spending a portion of each day in relaxed reading and study activity. Make learning a way of life and of living in your home.*

Parents should be aware that in addition to the physical environment the conversational atmosphere also teaches the child. Conversation in the home should be oriented toward education. Awareness of the esthetic delights of life comes naturally to a child who, even as an infant, hears the parents talking about music and art, or about authors and books, or hears the parents discuss events described in newspapers, or raise questions about issues or editorials in magazines. As children grow older, parents should include them in these serious conversations. Questions directed to the child will improve the child's self-image and, thus, the self-worth, because he or she was included in the conversation. *Above all, never "talk down" to the child.*

Parents can teach citizenship in the home by being active in the affairs of their local, county, state, or national government. Talk about politics and public issues, and encourage your children to think about public matters. Help your children learn to think constructively and critically by including them in your reading and discussion. Teach good citizenship by your actions in the home and the community. Such actions will teach as much as (maybe even more than) all the theory your children could study.

ACTION-ORIENTED GUIDELINES

As you begin to think in terms of teaching and learning, watch for suitable teaching moments. Use real life situations to illustrate your teaching about critical thinking and moral values. Following are some general guidelines to help you as you make your home function as your child's classroom away from school:

1. Make each experience in your home a learning opportunity for the child, but avoid giving all of the answers. Integrate a few key words here and there in your discussion to generate interest, then let the child draw his or her own conclusions.

2. Family experiences (such as business trips in which the father or mother includes the entire family, or vacations) can serve as excellent opportunities for teaching and learning. Even short excursions to the grocery store or across town can become as ideal an opportunity to present a new encounter to the child as can cross-country jaunts. Education and travel can be conjoined into a pleasurable learning experience if parents use every opportunity to enhance learning.

3. The wise parent is careful to avoid indoctrination. Your life's work need not be imposed on your child, and your political views should be expressed in such a manner that they show respect for the opposition party or candidate. Your biases and preconceived ideas can unduly and unfairly distort your child's thoughts unless you are careful not to thrust them at the child without giving them scrupulous consideration first.

4. Teach truth and moral values in a way that expresses tolerance for others and recognizes the many beliefs of others. If your child picks up "gutter" talk about any ethnic or minority group, casually say the proper name of the group and then tell the child a few of the attributes of these people. Show tolerance, compassion, and respect by actually living what you say. Teach consideration of others' beliefs and feelings by always being considerate of them yourself.

5. Be careful not to destroy your child's confidence in his or her school and teachers. Even though you may think that a particular teacher is not doing the best job of teaching, show some

support for that teacher to your child by finding something positive to say about him or her. The teacher merits your support while teaching your child.

6. Among the do's and don'ts of this book should be included caution to some parents to overcome any habitual conversation that frequently expresses negative opinions. A cheerful greeting of "Hello, isn't this a beautiful day?" should not be deflated with "Yes, but wait until tomorrow!" Children instinctively sense these attitudes in their parents and quickly adopt them as their own. If you deal in "negative-oriented" conversations, your child could very well grow up with this same inclination toward negativism. Make your conversations in the presence of your child, or to the child, have a positive message; make them uplifting to everyone's spirits.

Parents' actions teach respect or disrespect for law and authority. If you pay your taxes grudgingly (as most of us do) in the presence of your child, or if you attack the first-of-the-month bill paying with fury at the high cost of living, your child will feel that this is the proper way to behave when handing over hard-earned money. Teach that paying an honest debt is a natural part of living in this world and your child will learn honesty in financial dealings. The child will note with pride this exemplary conduct and will aspire to match it.

Obey traffic laws when driving or walking on public streets, and speak cordially to and positively about public servants such as policemen, firemen, postal employees, or trash collectors. Teach love and respect for all fellow humans by "living" the standards that you want your child to aspire to.

HOW TO LISTEN TO YOUR CHILDREN*

Learn to listen to your children. Never be so omniscient that your boy or girl cannot interject an opinion, and never ridicule the opinion. There may be times when you will counsel the child if you see that the opinion has come from a biased or bigoted associate. But the time-honored, heart-to-heart conversation between

---

*For more detailed information on listening skills, see chapters 3, 4, and 5 of Dr. Thomas Gordon's book, *Parent Effectiveness Training* (New York: The New American Library, Inc., 1975).

parent and child will let you reap vast returns as you watch your child mature into a fair-minded individual. Approach bias and bigotry with calm assurance, letting the child know that everyone is entitled to his or her opinion but that sometimes viewpoints are influenced by biases when all the facts are not known. Explain several sides of the issue to your child and guide him or her toward self-examination of the feelings and attitudes that have developed. For example:

> Your son comes home from school (or in from play) and calmly announces, "Jason's a cripple."
> "What do you mean by 'cripple'?" you ask, knowing that the word has never been used in your house.
> "Well, he stutters, he's a Negro, and Fred told me that black people stutter because their minds don't work well."
> "Let's think for a minute about what you just said," you answer quickly. "Your older sister, Jane, had a problem with stuttering and you know that she has almost a straight A average. Her mind seems to work very well, but she had a stuttering problem."
> "I didn't think of that," your son answers.
> "The other thing you said needs some more thought. You can't believe that black people have inferior minds. Some of the greatest scientists, artists, and leaders in our nation are Negroes. You will find many people with all kinds of ability and with superior minds coming from every race and nationality. Try to think fairly when friends like Fred say unfair things about others. Ask yourself if it is true, if it is clear thinking, and if there is any proof."

The foregoing example describes just one of the many typical opportunities you will have to teach fairness and help your child grow up free from prejudice. It takes many conversations like the example above. Don't let incidents like this one go by without offering a fine lesson while interest is high and the time is ripe to make your point.

Be an attentive parent. Listening can be a great asset to you as a parent. Get to know your child through conversation. Learn how to help your child through listening. Teach your child that you care through listening. Help your child to build a good self-image through listening. Let your child know that he or she can come to you when there is a crisis in his or her life by practicing the listening habit and by being a true counselor and friend.

As a general rule, most parents get so deeply involved in telling their children what to do that they forget to listen. As you strive to be an effective parent, you must know what your child is thinking. This comes from careful, patient listening. Following are some helpful hints:

1. You must understand your child if you are to have an effective influence. You keep the lines of communication open when you listen *actively.* Don't just *appear* to be listening; listen with active attention in order to learn.

2. Most children love to talk—especially if they feel free to express their views. Behave in a manner that will encourage conversation.

3. Use words in your conversation that invite further expression. Be sympathetic to the child's feelings and remember that these *feelings are important facts to you.* Use words of encouragement such as: "That sounds interesting, tell me more." "I understand how you must feel, but let's talk about it some more."

4. You should avoid playing your disciplinarian-guardian role so heavily and so constantly that you shut off some of the true inner feelings of your child. This is an important point to remember at any age, but it is particularly critical to remember this as you relate to your teenage children. We all dislike being lectured and admonished. Don't shut off conversation in this way.

5. Your child's conversations with you must be *genuine.* Beware of trivial responses that indicate only half awareness. Respond with comments that are relevant and, from the child's viewpoint, demonstrate understanding and concern.

6. Try to review the *content* and *frequency* of the conversations with your child. Try to find time—at least once each week—when you can have a conversation *in depth,* during which you encourage your child's expressions to deepen your understanding and help you to become more effective in your role. Respond sufficiently to stimulate expressions from your child but do not dominate or direct the conversation. Many parents hear

only what the child wants to express about his or her feelings and views, because the parent imposes opinions too freely and makes value judgments too early in the conversation. "Preachy" parents who lecture and admonish have difficulty in conversations with their children because they structure the conversation around their own values and concerns. Such parents are handicapped because of their limited skills in listening and conversing. True exchanges in depth will come only if your child has regular, *extensive* discussions with you. Superficial chats and short exchanges of a few words will not do.

7. Be alert to a new need for conversation. A troubled child needs to talk. Watch for signs that tell you that it is time to make a special effort to be close to your child. While avoiding being pushy or domineering, try to help your troubled child to share with you. You may learn some facts that will avoid deeper and more serious future problems. There are certain times of stress and crisis in the life of your child when your conversation and counsel will be needed. If you are psychologically close to your child and have a special parent-child rapport, you will detect these times easily and will be "let inside" of your child's inner thoughts and fears. At these times when you are needed the most, you will then be able to help.

WORKING WITH YOUR CHILD'S SCHOOL

If a parent wants a child to know that there is genuine interest and support for educational success, these must be manifested in a knowledge about the child's teachers, conditions at school, subjects that are causing difficulties, and many other matters of central concern to the child. It is an act of hypocrisy that is readily recognized by the child to give lip service to education and to know almost nothing about the child and the conditions of his or her schooling.

Parents must demonstrate interest. To express support with words and at the same time to show neglect by lack of active concern is to kill the child's motivation to learn. Report card time must be a matter of intense interest on the part of parents. Children must feel that progress at school is foremost in the minds of parents. A report card from school must be the topic of a long and earnest conversation. Academic marks should be discussed in an atmosphere of positive concern. Days present and absent should be reviewed. Any tardies marked on the card should be noted and discussed. Citizenship marks should receive a careful review.

The total program of studies can be discussed at each report card date. Parents should ask the child how they might help. Report card time needs to be a time of review and appraisal of progress and a goal-setting time for the next marking period.

Parents should get in touch with teachers immediately when there are danger signals transmitted through the report card. The views of both teacher and child should be weighed. Parents often learn many valuable facts from a teacher interview at school. Children should know when the interview will take place, and the results should be discussed with the child following the interview.

In the chapters that follow, the ideal situation will often be described as a model for the reader. This is not to ignore the fact that there are many real life problems that do not fit the pattern. You may find it difficult to talk to your child's teacher. Most teachers are anxious to meet with parents to discuss ways of developing closer cooperation between home and school. But there are problem situations that are beyond the control of the parent, and some of these stem from lack of teacher interest and competence.

DEALING WITH PROBLEM TEACHERS

What should parents do when they feel that their child is being taught by an incompetent? This is an age-old question that has troubled parents for years. The first response to this question must be one of caution to parents to be fair, open-minded, and objective in making judgments about teachers. Certainly parents should not remain silent if they are unhappy. Often, parents may not understand all the problems faced by a teacher in a given teaching situation. It is easy to make unwarranted conclusions. More than once, the author has observed parents arrange a transfer from one teacher to another only to find that they have in fact moved their child from a fully competent teacher to a marginally competent one. It is easy for parents to make erroneous judgments about teaching competence. You should be reluctant to ask for a transfer of your child on the basis of teacher incompetence. Following are some important considerations to guide parents' actions in dealing with what is perceived to be a problem teacher:

1. Avoid discussions in the presence of your child. Do not add to the problem by undermining the teacher.

2. Do all you can at home to compensate for the situation. Offer special tutoring help if possible.

3. If you are convinced that your child's teacher is not meeting your child's needs in the classroom, you should meet with the teacher. Discuss the problems as you see them. Try to learn about the teacher's problems. Be open-minded about the fact that part of the problem may be the fault of your child.

4. If you do not believe that the situation can be corrected by discussion and planning changes with the teacher, you should then meet with the school principal. Express your concerns calmly and objectively, and be sure to report your previous actions and conversations with the teacher. Be fair to the teacher, but describe your dissatisfaction in terms of your child's educational needs.

5. If you do not find an adequate solution after your conference with the principal, you may want to go to the school district headquarters office with your complaints.

6. You should remember that in most states there will be a school board member elected to represent your residential area on the board of education. If all your appeals fail to bring satisfaction, you are entitled to appeal the matter to the board member and on up to the total board. It is important in all of these appeals to remember that there are many students, numerous parents, and hundreds of problem situations. Be persistent and firm but do not make unreasonable demands. When you finally appeal to your school board member you should be sure that you have done all you can with the professional staff.

What about the lifestyle, the emotional climate, and the interpersonal relationships of members of your family? Are you relaxed, supportive, and noncompetitive with each other? Below you will find a description of the ten characteristics of a family with high potential for educational achievement. It is highly unlikely that any family you know would reach the ideal described in these ten points, so you should not feel discouraged if your family does not. This notwithstanding, you may be interested in these suggestions for improving the quality of your family life.

TEN CHARACTERISTICS OF A FAMILY WITH HIGH POTENTIAL FOR EDUCATION

From time to time a distinguished family is recognized for the outstanding accomplishments of all members. Some families seem to have unusual success. Every child seems to be highly motivated, well adjusted, and distinguished insofar as accomplishments are concerned. What are the characteristics of these unusual families? What do families do and what practices do parents encourage in the home that lead to these unusual accomplishments? Obviously, there are no simple formulas. But we do know from our observations and from comments offered by members of such families that there are some fundamental guidelines which enhance probability for success. Following are ten such guidelines that may be helpful to families for evaluating and improving the quality of family life. (It is important to emphasize that not many families meet all of these guidelines. You should not feel discouraged if you fall short of the ideal but recognize that all families have need to make improvements.)

1. *The family is deeply involved in learning* This involvement includes continuous conversation about learning and about topics that stimulate the mind and generate an overall desire to acquire knowledge and to be intellectually competent. Before, during, and after school the children from such families are oriented toward intellectual activity. There is strong encouragement and stimulation toward thinking and toward utilizing the mind in seeking lofty goals and in perpetuating high ideals.

2. *The family is psychologically close.* There is an atmosphere in the home of warmth and caring for each other. The members of the family identify as a family unit. This psychological closeness is usually created by a large number of family-type activities. This lifestyle is contrasted with many aspects of modern-day family life where each member goes his own way and sees the home only as a place for sleeping and eating. The family members have a genuine regard for each other and a feeling of

responsibility toward the family and toward helping others to reach goals and the feeling of fulfillment.

3. *The family members are oriented toward the neighborhood and community.* They make contributions to others less fortunate than they. The family members give of themselves when no particular reward is expected. In addition to meeting their own needs as individual family members, they are actively involved in helping others and in participating in community activities that tend to lift up the less fortunate.

4. *The children in the family largely govern themselves and settle problems among themselves with very little parental intervention.* Personality conflicts are few in such families. Talking and exchanging of ideas among brothers and sisters seem to help this self-governance characteristic. Rare is the case where a dispute has to be arbitrated by the father or the mother.

5. *The conversation among family members is quite clear and spontaneous.* The family members speak freely and have a sense of openness and a lack of tension in conversation. The children grow up in a family atmosphere where clear expression and spontaneous relating of one's thoughts and feelings are encouraged. Communication among family members is, of course, very important. The achieving family encourages this free expression and establishes a pattern of living and a sense of emotional interrelatedness that make this free expression easily attained.

6. *The conversation is generally constructive.* Most of the comments made by family members to each other are positive. This all reflects a certain maturity and understanding among the family members. There is a sense of duty and willingness to contribute toward a constructive emotional climate in the home. Encouragement is offered to each other. Even criticism is framed in positive ways. The conversation is oriented toward placing the needs and the well-being of the other person very high in the hierarchy of values. This attitude offers a considerable amount of reinforcement for good behavior and for positive thinking in the home.

7. *There is very little distortion in the conversation.* Family members tend to tell things as they are. They don't make problems more than they need to or exaggerate them for sake of

emphasis. Conversely, the family members tend to be modest and the ego-seeking is low key. This approach provides healthy reality therapy on a continuous basis for children growing up.

8. *The parents hear differences of opinion and behave toward children in a way that will encourage expressions of differences.* Through this listening to differences of opinion and through this approach that does not compel agreement, the parents are able to detect problems as they surface from conversations. This openness to hear differences is encouraged by the aspect of number 7 by keeping distortion to a minimum and by letting children know that parental egos need no feeding because the level of maturity is beyond this need.

9. *The life history of family members during the growing time is one of increasing independence with age.* There is a gradual taking on of more work, added responsibility, and independent decision-making opportunity. Each member of the family feels that it is natural for those older and more mature to have more privileges and also more responsibilities. This gradual transition toward independence is very important and is a characteristic of family life that should be encouraged.

10. *Both the father and the mother are very active participators in family affairs.* One of the parents will act as the hearing examiner on serious difficulties. Both parents have a rapport with all members of the family that communicates interest, strong support, and an active orientation toward the family as one of the central purposes of their lives. The parents are a source of stability and strength to the family members. They act as heads of the family more in the sense of being a source of support, understanding, and encouragement. Most of the decisions in the home are cooperative ones which the parents share extensively before decisions are made. This helps to build family identity and family concern for working together in a way that will make major decisions correct and wise actions on the part of the entire family.

Most active families will be able to add to this list of ten guidelines for success. Little has been said, for example, about hard work, moral values, and ideals. However, they are reflected in all that is implied in these guidelines. To be sure, a successful family needs deep spiritual roots with religious and moral values that bring stability and a feeling of direction and purpose in living. The foregoing list of guidelines attempts to communicate the emotional relationships and the psychological climate that must guide a family that is supportive of the schools and of educational activities. Children who grow up in this type of climate have a great potential for developing most of the latent talents and capacities with which they have been genetically endowed.

THE CHARACTERISTICS OF A HEALTHY PERSONALITY

One of the big challenges facing both the home and the school is to provide optimum opportunities for children to develop healthy personalities. A healthy personality reflects on attitudes and relationships that one child will have with another. It reflects acceptance of the normal problems and difficulties of living in today's world. It reflects a good balance between too much pressure and not enough drive and self-commitment. What are the characteristics of a youth who is well-adjusted and is personable and outgoing? What are the attributes of a young person possessed of a truly healthy personality? Parents should be studying the attitudinal and personality development of their children. The following are twelve characteristics of a school-age boy or girl with this so-called healthy personality:

1. *The healthy personality displays a stable disposition most of the time.* This individual has, of course, bad moments and periods of time when moods reflect the same. But the individual is usually of an even temperament that is free from moodiness.

2. *The person with a healthy personality is generally nondefensive about criticism.* The ability not to overreact when criticism is expressed is a sign of emotional stability and maturity. Persons committed to self-improvement are generally introspective. Such individuals usually accept ideas that will help them to improve. They can take criticism for what it is worth without responding defensively.

3. *The person possessed of a healthy personality is generally realistic about his or her capabilities.* This individual makes down-to-earth decisions that reflect maturity and a solid appraisal of what can and cannot be accomplished.

4. *The personable individual is generally able to discipline himself or herself.* This individual learns to do what should be done and has the capacity of making choices relative to what is necessary and what is not always pleasurable, and of resisting impulses. We all must learn how to deny ourselves certain wants that are not good for us. Young people must learn self-discipline. One of the greatest conquests in life is to conquer oneself and to let reason and logic rule desires and appetites.

5. *The well-adjusted and personable individual knows how to make distinctions between small matters and major items of concern.* This person does not let little things bother him. Young people need to learn this great lesson as early in life as possible. With all the frustrations and difficulties with which one has to contend in the modern world it is easy to get uptight with the everyday frustrations of living. The person with a healthy personality knows how to identify the big things and how to sort out the items that are not of sufficient consequence to generate emotions that use up energy, time, and talent.

6. *A good sense of humor is vital to the well-adjusted individual.* It is particularly important to learn not to take oneself too seriously. We all need to develop the capacity to laugh at jokes that are on ourselves as well as jokes that are on others.

7. *The well-adjusted individual has the ability to feel for others and to have compassion for the problems and difficulties of fellow human beings.* This individual is sensitive and understanding. The capability to project oneself into the being of another is essential to becoming a warm and compassionate person. Empathy and lack of self-centeredness are personality traits that should be sought by our youth. Parents should help children to develop this capacity by practicing it in the home and by pointing out how essential this warm human trait is for all of us and for the world in general.

8. *Generally speaking, the big decisions and the deliberations leading up to making them do not unduly frustrate the well-adjusted person.* It is important to be able to make important decisions when they need to be made without too much fuss and fretting. Children need to be taught to make their own decisions, and they need to learn how to analyze various alternatives and come up with a decision in a timely manner.

9. *A person with a healthy personality is inner-directed.* This person has his or her own values and lives by them. Such an individual is not easily swayed by the crowd. Decisions are made according to values and according to personal choices that come from within the individual and not from outside pressures and popular influences. Parents need to help children to recognize the value of this personality trait and to encourage a lifestyle that leads to attainment of the same.

10. *A mature individual and one without personality maladjustments has learned to be frugal.* Wastefulness and failure to set priorities in spending money and in spending time are all characteristics of emotionally disturbed and maladjusted persons. The mature, self-directed individual gets satisfaction from other than material things. In guiding the values and attitudes of children, parents should teach priorities in spending both time and money. Parents should lead children to recognize the great virtue of following priorities and taking care of first things first. Individuals who impulsively spend money, or their time, in a way that does not reflect mature judgment are certainly persons who are going to live unhappy lives, will be frustrated, and will not find the joy and fulfillment that life can give. Much thoughtful consideration needs to be given to this personality attribute by parents seeking to guide children along the right path to maturity.

11. *Well-adjusted individuals usually have plenty to do to occupy time.* A person with a healthy personality is usually highly involved in matters at home, in the neighborhood, at school, at church, and in the community. Such an individual is active and participates in and aggressively contributes to worthy endeavors. Parents should evaluate the degree of involvement that each child has in school, church, and community activities. Intense activity in these areas leads a child away from emotional difficulties and from self-centeredness. The best life is a contributing life where one is constantly in the forefront of the serious problems faced by the community. The habit of commitment and the desire to pitch in and be an active part of school and community life must be cultivated by parents. Parents should watch for children who hang back and display reluctance to become a part of activities. With real tact and a certain amount of gentle encouragement many students inclined toward a life of isolation and noncommitment can be led in the right direction.

12. *A person possessed of a healthy personality has many friends.* This individual can make friends easily. This individual relates to others and can participate in a group feeling free and easy. Social competence and an outgoing personality seem to go hand in hand. At an early age, parents should lead children to reach out to their peers and make lasting friendships. This comes quite naturally in many children, but it often needs to be deliberately nurtured in certain personality types. Parents can often sponsor activities and create situations where this capacity can be developed in a very natural and free setting.

THE HOME'S INFLUENCE ON PERSONALITY

Certainly the home and the family setting contribute more to the development of personality and to the unfolding of the desired capabilities described above in a much more dynamic and relevant way than does the school. This is not to say that these attributes cannot and should not be developed at school. It is to say that parents, brothers and sisters, and the home setting contribute much more in this area of human development than does the school. Many of these personality characteristics have been developed prior to the time that a child enters school. At least the inclinations toward certain personality attributes are unfolding long before school age is reached. That is why parents should have in mind the components of a good, healthy personality.

The foregoing list of twelve attributes is not, of course, exhaustive. But it does present a fairly good profile of an individual who is well-adjusted and personable. If parents are going to help children to develop those characteristics that we all admire in our fellow human beings, they must understand some of the key human inclinations that make up a total, healthy personality.

As a parent you should study this list and compare this admittedly ideal description with the personality traits and attributes of each child in the family. You should detect obvious deficiencies and seek ways of providing opportunities for growth and development in areas that are needed. It is quite common for parents to think that personality is some sort of vague and highly complex human attribute that cannot be defined and cannot be developed. Although the subject is admittedly complex, it is not difficult to define the attributes that we admire in others and to analyze ways in which we can improve the personality development opportunities of our children.

There can be little dispute about the fact that personality is influenced to some extent by heredity. Handsome, intelligent, well-endowed children have a great advantage. But haven't you known persons who were quite homely in physical appearance, who appeared at first to be lacking in many other respects, but who turned out to be very dynamic and highly personable individuals once you got to know them? There is great charm and power in a healthy personality. The prime responsibility for developing it must rest with the home and specifically with the parents.

You should be very conscious of how the home molds character and shapes personality. This is a creative process. Children lacking in inherited characteristics can greatly compensate for such limitations through developing a powerful personality. Most of the parent-sponsored activities described in this book will have a powerful influence on your child's personality. In this sense, you will have more influence in helping your child develop a winning personality by your study and application of all the principles advocated in the chapters that follow. You should help your child to develop those genuine, nonartificial winning ways that are attractive, magnetic, and outreaching to others. Teach this by experience and by the winning power of invitation to be all those things outlined in the discussion of the twelve personality characteristics. Teach it by love and encouragement. Be sure to teach it by dynamic example in the way you live and in the way you relate to others. Keep in mind that you are a model to children. Make sure that your examples are positive and that the life you live is one that will show and tell the child those things that must be shown and must be told.

If a child is to develop a stable disposition and avoid the extremes of mood and feeling, he or she must be nurtured in a home that reflects a serene and confident outlook toward life. If a child is to be nondefensive and to accept criticism in a positive way, he or she must live in an atmosphere that is accepting of criticism and is positive about self-improvement and responsiveness to feedback. If a child is going to learn to be highly involved in activities at home, at school, and in the neighborhood, he or she must live in a home that is oriented in this direction. A sense of humor is developed by living with a family that has a capacity for laughter and expressive joy. The capacity for making friends is nurtured in a home that enables friends to enjoy activities in that home. Moral and spiritual values that shape personality and attitude grow within the mind of the child who lives where there is a value system that reflects goodness, compassion, honesty, concern, and care for others.

Your example in real life circumstances will do much to formulate a healthy personality for your child. Your actions will speak to him every day with more eloquence and clarity than all the teaching that he can possibly receive at school. If you are to send your child to school and launch him into a happy and self-fulfilling life, build his personality and character at home by your own actions. Trite as it may sound, actions truly speak louder than words. Your child will be a product of these actions and of the dynamic living example that you provide for him.

SINGLE PARENTS

In many homes a mother or father faces the task of parenthood alone. Either through death or divorce, single parent heads of families are quite common. A single parent must, of course, try to compensate for what children miss when being raised by a mother only or by a father without a mother. This situation calls for an optimistic attitude. The single parent can still do many of the things advocated in this book if there is sufficient commitment and tenacity. This is not to say that it is easy, but the task is far from impossible. The author was reared in a home by a widowed mother who also had responsibility for eight other children. Many of the ten characteristics earlier described for a successful family were present in this home because of the great spirit of a widow with a will to succeed as a single parent.

While the chapters that follow will discuss the work and techniques of married parents living together with their children, application of many recommended practices for a single-parent family will be apparent to readers carrying these burdens.

In this chapter we have discussed the general impact of family life on learning. The child's home environment is possibly more conclusive than any other factor in shaping a winning personality and a positive attitude. You should, in your efforts to enhance the learning of your child, review often the following items in this chapter: (1) the discussion of the learning atmosphere, (2) the six general action-oriented guidelines, (3) the seven helpful hints on listening, (4) the discussion about working with your child's school, (5) the ten characteristics of a family with high potential for learning, and (6) the twelve characteristics of a healthy personality. As you do this, you will be reminded of the need to be an active, concerned parent. You will have some check list items against which you may measure your progress as you move along in the pleasurable task of guiding and teaching your children in a fully committed and powerfully influential home.

It is hoped that this first chapter has helped you to realize that you are already well on your way to providing the learning climate that your child needs in your home. The basic ideas are easy to understand and to apply in your home situation. If you have discovered a few aspects of the home environment that should be changed, you should not be discouraged because few families measure up to all these ideals. The gap between what is and what ought to be in your home will be more easily closed as you read and apply the information about motivating children and building a positive self-image.

2.
Motivation and Self-Image: The Keys to Success in School

Actively concerned parents should understand the nature of motivation. They should know how to appeal to the inner drive of children. As adults, we know that our personal motives have a great deal to do with our behavior. In addition to our intellectual judgments, our personal motives play a substantial role in what we do and why we do it.

If a child is to be successful in school, the child must have *inner drive* as well as outer stimulation and encouragement. The student must decide for himself or herself that learning is important and that schoolwork will lead to results that will be rewarding. There are both internal and external forces that cause a person to strive for particular ends and outcomes. We can offer rewards, encouragement, and praise as outer stimulation to induce children to seek those educational outcomes that will be beneficial to them; but we must also realize that attitudes are important, and that positive attitudes toward learning are formulated to a considerable extent by past experiences.

Parents should be as concerned about the means that lead to early accomplishment in a child's life as they are about the ends. Getting a child to do a certain task by force or by fear of punishment may promote the short-range ends that a parent is seeking, but attitudes will be formed that are damaging to the long-range development of the child. Therefore, especially in the early years of school, parents and teachers should seek to motivate the child through positive efforts, avoiding threats, coercion, and punishment as much as possible. The point to remember is that pressure and punishment must be used sparingly. We cannot avoid all pressure and all punishment; but if we are concerned about attitudes and about creating in the child an inner motivation to do those things we know ought to be done, we must strive to make sure that experiences are pleasant, rewarding, and useful in the eyes of the child.*

GUIDELINES ON MOTIVATION

One of the most important principles learned by teachers when they are training to become professional educators is that of motivation. Human beings usually respond to experiences in an emotional as well as in an intellectual way. Unpleasant experiences tend to cause us to shrink from them and strive to avoid repeating them. We form mental images about certain things that are associated with specific events that have occurred to us. For example, an adult who has had extreme difficulty in studying algebra may develop a deep-seated feeling of dread whenever the subject is mentioned. Past experience can cause a person to respond emotionally to anything that has to do with algebra. We can form the same attitudes toward people's names, toward colors, foods, and even games we play if we have had unpleasant or painful episodes associated with them. We form attitudes about and automatic responses to unpleasant experiences that occur repeatedly. Eventually, no amount of logic, not even the clearest amount of intellectual insight, can totally erase these deeply ingrained negative feelings. It is important to recognize that your child's experiences today are shaping many attitudes and building automatic emotional responses that will affect inner motivation and ultimate

---

*For further reading on developing inner drive and a will to achieve see Thomas W. Evans' book, *The School in the Home* (New York: Harper and Row, 1973), especially chapters 7 and 8.

achievement. We should strive to use these attitude shaping experiences to the child's advantage.

Our attitudes are formed by the kind of motivation we get from the activities and occurrences that touch our lives. As we seek to motivate children to learn, we must try to avoid the formation of negative attitudes by attempting to create conditions that will buttress, in a positive manner, the child's learning activities in the home. *There is likely no other principle of teaching and learning that is more significant than the simple concept of being positive and of making sure that early life experiences shape a positive self-image for the child. Feelings of self-worth come early and they are shaped by experience. There must be constant awareness that early experiences should be successful and therefore rewarding to the child. Rebellion and dislike for learning will be the result if this paramount principle is ignored. A child's self-concept, attitudes toward life, and ability to learn will be largely formed by your approach as a parent.*

It is imperative that parents learn to apply sound principles that will help the child develop a healthy compulsion to be a successful learner at home and at school.* Because most humans persist in doing those things that are rewarding and pleasurable, parents should make those first teaching experiences happy and successful.

A motivation-conscious parent will be immensely careful about using negative responses that could condition the child to build attitudes that could become barriers to learning in future life. Even in difficult learning activity and study, there must be rewards that reinforce and give encouragement for future effort. The child must have a sense of accomplishment and progress. During particularly difficult times in a child's educational life, it is important to encourage and to give hope. It is highly desirable to instill confidence and to offer support. We must do this, of course, in a positive and genuine way. Our rewards and the praise we offer must be sincere and meaningful if they are to accomplish the desirable ends we are seeking.

It is even more important to make sure that the child is faced with a task where success is not only possible but highly probable. Be sure that the task is obtainable from the perspective of the child's abilities. More children are turned off by being

---

*For a stimulating and easy to understand reference on the impact of experience on intelligence, see J. McV. Hunt's book, *Intelligence and Experience* (New York: The Ronald Press Co., 1961).

confronted with enormously difficult tasks than by any other approach. The challenge can be too easy as well as too difficult, but it is more often the latter. Most educational psychologists agree that a child, when working seriously at a learning task, should be responding correctly to about eight out of every ten learning items. If the child is not making some mistakes, the task is too easy. But if the child is missing many more than eight out of ten items attempted, the task is too difficult and deep discouragement and negative reactions will soon occur. This is a good guideline to remember in working with your child.

Parents too often ignore the emotional aspects of their child's responses to learning. They try to use logic to overcome attitudes that have been formed through the years as a result of repeated negative experience. The child's experiences often create such strong emotional responses and deep-seated negative attitudes that no amount of parent logic can reverse them.

It is important for parents to remember that learning results from almost all experiences that a child has. Children are forming attitudes from experiences that condition them to respond emotionally and also from those that help them form attitudes not necessarily based on logic but on emotional responses to similar past occurrences. Keeping this in mind, we should avoid offering rewards or encouragement for repetition of actions that we know are not useful and desirable for the child.

As parents work with their children in the home, they must seek activities that can promise success for their offspring. Most of the "work" a child does around the house should be structured in such a way that success and relative ease of accomplishment are possible. Too much failure discourages the child from wanting to try again. Conversely, success rewards the child's attempts and leads the child to move ahead to accomplish more. *Success is contagious in that it prompts additional attempts, and these lead to more progress.*

If a parent is teaching the child how to perform a task that will require a length of time to learn, the task should be presented step by step so that the total job does not seem too forbidding to the child. The old expression that the first step in eating an elephant is to cut it up into little pieces applies here. Assignments should be broken down into small pieces, and the child should be allowed to proceed from one simple step to the next, with most of the trials being successful. The child will then have a sense of momentum, of progress, and the accomplishment in itself will be rewarding and stimulating.

The child whose home atmosphere is tempered to promote success and pleasure from learning experiences will likely develop a positive, "can do" attitude. This creates a personality that is supported by an attitude and an expectation of success. We teach through experience more than we teach by words. The child who experiences success is confident. A child cannot attain this attitude merely by being taught about success. Success must actually be experienced in most of the attempts that the child makes. We should remember, of course, that some failure should be expected and is actually necessary. But the golden rules of positive reinforcement in learning tell us that about eight of every ten attempts should reward the child with the feeling of success that comes from knowing that the response was an accurate or correct one. The self-confidence and poise of the child are greatly influenced by these largely successful experiences. It is what we experience that touches our attitudes and shapes our personalities just as much as what we may have learned intellectually. The following episode illustrates this:

Since Mary had reached the age of ten, her mother required her to share in some of the kitchen chores. Mary enjoyed cooking. Her mother used this opportunity to teach Mary how to prepare meals and how to serve food with grace and good taste. Mother and daughter soon learned to share in building a recipe file. They enjoyed looking for new ideas in foods. This led to shopping at the supermarket and looking for good buys that would stretch the family budget. Mary's mother found many teaching opportunities.

On Sundays it was Mary's duty to clear the table and wash all the dishes. This was usually a fairly large job and Mary began to dread it. One Sunday after a large number of guests had departed, the task appeared so huge to Mary that she approached her usual Sunday afternoon duties with tears in her eyes. From the perspective of a ten-year-old this was an enormous mountain of work.

Mary's mother wisely agreed to help. But she did so in recognition of Mary's past assistance to her. She tried to make the job more pleasant by tuning in Mary's favorite music while they labored together. When the job was finished she praised Mary for being so grown-up in doing her duties, and she offered an extra privilege to Mary as further recognition of her work.

Mary's mother was wise in not releasing her daughter from her regular duties. She was also wise in making the big task more palatable. She applied the principles of motivation while the work was in progress by providing pleasant music and in the rewards that were offered after the work was completed.

Some parents mistakenly take a hard line. They insist that the entire task be done without any help and without praise or reward. Such parents feel that a get-tough attitude will strengthen character and show without question what is expected.

Other parents would go to the opposite extreme and let the child off without any effort at the first sign of tears. Then they would scold and complain that the child was immature and a burden for not doing her share of the work.

Parental behavior must be consistent. It must be constructive in building a positive self-image, and it must reward and encourage. Such behavior teaches ... it shapes attitudes and leads to success in endeavors at school.

A child cannot learn about love and how to grow to be a healthy, happy, and well-adjusted adult by just being taught about love. He or she must experience it in the home, beginning in the early years of life. *A child cannot learn to exert a great amount of drive and energy toward being academically successful in school by being taught about academic success and by being admonished that he or she should be successful. The child must actually experience this success.* The success must be part of the child's life, must be part of the memories of past experience, and must largely color the present attitude that goes into the immediate task of taking on a new learning experience at home and at school. The only way to learn to function successfully is to experience success. Any person approaching a new task brings to this challenge all of his past experiences. Before actually engaging in the new learning experience, the child actually lives in his mind what the experience is going to be like, often imagining it vividly and in considerable detail. The child's entire nervous system comes into play as a new learning challenge is approached. By bringing a positive self-image and a strong "can do" attitude that has been built through the years in a home that is dedicated to building solid, reinforcing experiences for children, the child anticipates the new task with considerable joy and with a great amount of confidence that the new experiences will be successful.

It is helpful to remember the old Chinese proverb that the longest journey begins with the first step. Parents mustn't point out how long the entire task is going to take as they bring their child to a new phase in her educational lifetime. They should let the child take a few tentative steps and feel the rewards that come from successful explorations. She then can move on gradually, a step at a time, through the total process. Often we point out the totality of a task at the outset, and it appears too formidable to the child. Preferably we should move her step by step along the pathway, letting her enjoy progress in a natural way. Before she is aware of it, the long and arduous task has been accomplished, and she has been spared the feeling of dread she might feel if first confronted with what she considered an enormous venture.

BUT WHAT ABOUT PUNISHMENT?

Inevitably, a certain amount of pressure and mild punishment should be applied in many homes with many children. When a child must be punished, the reason for the punishment should be well understood. The unpleasant experience should be carried out forthwith so that the child equates the punishment with the misdeed. Following this, loving attention should be given to allay any guilt feelings or resentment that may have arisen in the child. Although failure, punishment, pain, and misery are the inevitable consequences of misconduct or misunderstandings, they should be a lesser part of life. Living in a home where such occurrences are short-lived and quickly replaced by positive, pleasant, and reinforcing experiences will enhance a child's outlook on life. Parents with a positive outlook will consistently provide the kind of reinforcement and motivation in the home which will do much toward helping their child attain the ends they seek.

REVIEWING AND EVALUATING THE MOTIVATIONAL CLIMATE

Parents should confer with each other frequently about the emotional and attitudinal climate of the home. They should ask themselves if the atmosphere and general outlook are positive and reinforcing. They should provide methods for giving encouragement, hope, support, rewards, and overall stimulation to their children. They should have earnest conversations with their children to elicit each child's attitudes and thoughts. From this they can develop the keys to new strategies that can lead to more successful parenting. They should study the children's fears as well as their aspirations so that they are able to develop such strategies. And they should resolve constantly to improve the overall impact of the home to build a motivational climate that will lead to academic success and true happiness for each child in the family.

If parents remember that their children's feelings about learning are clues to their learning advancement, they can strive to be more ingenious parents. Happy moods and healthy attitudes at home and school are as important as high IQ's. We must begin early to attain these desirable attitudes. Parents shouldn't let weeks or months go by without constantly evaluating the motivational climate in their home and what it is doing to build a good self-image and a success-oriented outlook so necessary in all human beings. From their loving concern and understanding support will grow constant improvement in their effectiveness as parents. Motivation, understanding attitudes, and application of reinforcement principles are the great keys to success.

BUILDING A POSITIVE SELF-IMAGE

The key idea of the foregoing discussion is that a student's self-concepts and feelings of self-worth are very closely tied to what experience has taught him. The student must experience success in his early years. He must feel worthy and confident. His overall judgment of himself must be sufficiently high so that he will know he can accomplish the things that he aspires to attain.

Parents must constantly make sure that each child in the family receives some of the recognition and attention that all human beings need for a sense of worthiness. As a parent, this is one of your prime responsibilities. This is your first duty as a person sharing educational responsibilities with the school. Send your child to school with a positive self-image, and the first big step to success will have been attained.

How does one do this? Following are four guidelines to helping your child build a positive self-image:

1. First of all your child must feel your genuine love and respect. Put your child high in your priorities. Your child needs *you*—not a hired babysitter in the home. Make sure that your social commitments and your work do not rob your child of the right to be *first* in the priorities you have for using your time. Be sure that your children know that you care for them. Demonstrate

this by the way that you give of yourself in expressing your love, encouragement, and concern for your children.

2. Be conscious of what your conversation does to build up or tear down the self. Just as 80 percent of a child's efforts in study and learning should be successful, so should your conversation be positive. Make sure that your conversation builds the self-concept. It is easy to be so eager to lead a child to perfection that we correct too much. In correcting and leading, be positive and encouraging rather than critical and negative.

3. Take time to review in your mind the number of positive, self-concept building remarks that you have directed toward your child. It is a good idea even to inventory your conversational approaches to your child. If you remember being negative too much, perhaps you are more nervous and tense than you should be about your child's behavior. Study *yourself* and *your* relationship with your child to make sure that you have established the positive "can do" approach.

4. Watch the competitive relationships your child has with others in the home and neighborhood. If your child is "put down" too much by others you may be headed for trouble. Without being too protective set up success situations when the stress is heavy and your child's image is a bit droopy. Care must be exercised that these experiences are not contrived and phony. They need not be if you are aware of the strengths of your child and can genuinely draw out the display of something that the child can do well.

The following episode illustrates how parents can intervene to help a child find his own place and build feelings of self-worth:

Bill's older brother was an outstanding athlete. His father was a sports enthusiast. The older brother received so much praise and attention because of his athletic prowess that Bill tried to emulate him. But Bill had little talent for sports. His physical stature, his temperament, and his overall talents made it obvious that he could never match his brother's accomplishments in sports.

After many disastrous attempts, Bill withdrew from all sports participation. Moreover, he began to display fits of jealousy. He would look for opportunities to criticize his brother. He refused to attend events in which his brother was on display. He started to withdraw from all activities in the family. He was very anxious to avoid any competitive situation. Although he never admitted it, deep down he felt that he was inferior to his brother. He also believed that his father looked upon him as an inferior person.

Bill's mother very astutely followed his gradual shift in attitude and outward personality. She convinced Bill's father that they would soon have a serious problem if they did not find a means to help Bill show some distinctive talent.

Bill was, at one time, interested in art. But he dropped his activity in this area after his older brother labeled his attempts as "sissy stuff." Bill was also an able student with an obviously good mind.

Following several months of careful preparation, Bill's mother persuaded him to enroll in an arts and crafts club at school. He also enrolled in a special after-school creative writing class.

Within the next year Bill had won an honorable mention in a school-sponsored art show. Two articles he had written were published in the school magazine.

Bill's parents tried to give him full recognition and genuine praise for his accomplishments. This recognition greatly enhanced Bill's feelings of self-worth. After months of inner turmoil and frustration, his attitude changed. He started to come out of his shell and the cloud of negative feeling that had surrounded him.

This was a turning point in Bill's life. He weathered a crisis because a wise and insightful mother recognized a problem and took action to fill a need.

WATCHING FOR CHILD-PERCEIVED DISASTERS

A series of events in a child's life that are defeating and negative must be offset by self-fulfilling experiences. Wise parents will observe these critical phases in the child's life and help when the need is great. Be aware of your child's disappointments at school and be cognizant of losses of valued possessions that may cause a great feeling of depression and loss. Students are often hurt by peer-group actions. Your child may not gain favor in a social circle or in a club. Your child may lose or damage an item that is prized very highly. Such experiences are normal in all our lives. Most children get through these rough spots without undue harm to the personality. We must be wise in knowing when to help and when to leave the child on his or her own. Too much help and protection can be damaging, and the child will not learn to cope with the normal stresses and disappointments that are part of life and living.

But be alert for the series of unfortunate events that can come one after another. The near catastrophes need our attention and concern as parents. You need to keep the spark and spirit of self-concept alive in these critical periods when life's fortunes seem to be falling apart insofar as the child is concerned. The teenage years are especially critical in this regard. Be close to your child during this time. Events beyond your comprehension may be striking at your son or daughter. You may respond to behavior in a way that adds to problems and tears away at the self-concept at a very crucial period. The important thing to remember, especially during the teenage years, is that there are many emotional, self-concept tearing situations that develop almost daily in the child's life. Some of these matters may seem trivial to you but they are deeply important to the teenager. Be particularly sensitive and sympathetic during this time if you want to preserve your child's self-image and build the self-concept.

Above all, try to help your child avoid seeing himself or herself as a born loser. The child who approaches a new situation or challenge expecting to fail is a child in deep trouble at home and at school. If you detect this situation in your child's outlook and personality, be sure to enlist the assistance of the school. How to seek this help is described in subsequent chapters of this book. But good insurance against this very difficult problem is to be in constant contact with your child and to be a diligent parent committed to building the self-image and "can do" attitude every month of your child's life.

THE PARENT'S RESPONSIBILITY FOR CHILD SELF-CONCEPT

The human being's self-concept is almost all pervasive. Almost all success and failure begin with this image that one has of oneself. All other people with whom we have contact add to or detract from this self-concept; but no one can add so much or detract so powerfully as the parent. If one has had many successes in life, one approaches a new situation with the expectation that one will succeed again. This confidence in the self gives all of us courage to keep trying and to face life with optimism and with deep inner self-assurance.

MOTIVATION AND SELF-IMAGE

Many studies of student achievement and motivation in school have proven that the self-concept is a great predictor of success in school. Help your child to be successful at school by fostering success and a "can do" attitude at home. A student's *belief* in how well he will achieve in a class at school is highly correlated with that student's *actual* achievement. The successful student comes to school filled with enthusiasm and expectations of success that parents have helped to build at home. This is what motivation is all about. It starts with you as a parent and it ends with your child moving into the world after high school graduation filled with confidence in his or her future and ability to succeed in any challenge met. Remember the following four points as you help your child build a positive self-image:

1. You must be sincere in your behavior and in your actions to help your child to be oriented toward success.

2. Don't be a manipulator.

3. Be sincere in your praise.

4. Be positive most of the time in your contact.

This all begins, of course, with your own attitude toward yourself as well as toward your family members. Before any of us as parents can help our children to feel good about *themselves*, we must feel good about *ourselves*.

Are you overwhelmed at this point with all that you should be doing or with all the things that you are doing that may be wrong? Not many parents accomplish all the objectives advocated in this chapter. These are the ideal circumstances for providing motivation for learning and for establishing an environment that builds a positive self-image. And not many meet the ideal, so, again, you should not be discouraged if you do not. Try to identify a few attainable goals and then work gradually and systematically to reach them. But don't feel that you have to make a host of changes all at one time.

You may also have the impression that you are not able to find the time or learn all the facts necessary to become a capable parent and teacher. But, as we shall explain in the next chapter, this need not be the situation. You will need to master only a few simple concepts and develop some new basic ideas about your role as a teaching parent. Much of the time required will be time you already spend with your child in your daily routine. While you spend this time you will gradually learn to convert your typical experiences into teaching and learning opportunities. With little additional effort you should be able to convert your home into a much more powerful learning environment. This will be done through the *incidental teaching method* described in the next chapter.

3.
The Home-Based Curriculum and the Incidental Teaching Method

In the preface the point was emphasized that the parent is the child's first and most influential teacher and that the home is the first classroom. As a parent you must assume part of the responsibility for what your child learns. You should be actively concerned about increasing the capacity of your child's intellect. Early in your child's lifetime you should help him or her to learn how to learn.

In this chapter we will discuss the home-based curriculum and the incidental teaching method as we explain what to teach and describe how it should be taught. For purposes of this discussion the curriculum is the sum total of all learning experiences that are provided for the child at home and at school. The home-based curriculum includes those learning experiences that the parent should sponsor by using a special method called *incidental teaching*. In addition to describing this home-based teaching procedure, this chapter will offer some illustrations to demonstrate how you may use this teaching process in your daily routine as you work and play with your child. Then, in chapter five we will extend our discussion to the school curriculum and provide suggestions for enriching the curriculum in the home.

THE INCIDENTAL TEACHING METHOD

Incidental teaching requires an attitude, awareness, and readiness on your part to convert many of the routine experiences that you share with your child into opportunities for learning and intellectual growth. Learning occurs when interest is high and curiosity is aroused. Opportunities for incidental teaching occur continuously and in a most natural setting every day in your living experiences with your child. You need to recognize these opportunities that can be converted into productive learning experiences.

To illustrate the incidental teaching method we will describe the activities of a mother of a preschool child as she follows the routine of a typical day:

Mary is the mother of a three-year-old son, Peter. Their day's learning experiences begin as Mary enter's Peter's room after hearing the usual noises that he is awake and ready to get out of his bed.

"Good morning, Peter," Mary says as she greets her young son. "Let's go into the bathroom before you get dressed."

Mary takes her three-year-old to the bathroom. She remembers that he learned the word *hot* the previous day when he put his hand into some extra warm water as it was filling the bathtub. She decides to teach the words hot and cold by giving the child an opportunity to feel both cold and extra warm water as she gets ready to wash him before dressing for the day's activities. If Peter is interested and responsive she will spend some time with this teaching activity. It will all depend on how the first incidents occur.

Since Peter is learning many new words, Mary wants to stimulate his growing intellect and expand his vocabulary with every incident in the daily routine. *But she does not want to use pressure, to force any learning by drill, nor to keep the child from feeling relaxed and free to enjoy a carefree day with her.*

Mary has clearly in mind the new words she wants to teach, some new colors and some number concepts that should be learned next. She has a plan for the week. *But she will execute her teaching activities only in the natural sequence of events. She will teach incidentally rather than try to sit down and "hold school" in the formal, disciplined tradition of teaching. Her teaching opportunities will be many if she thinks about her responsibilities to nurture Peter's mind as she works, talks, laughs, and plays with him throughout the day.*

As Mary takes off Peter's undershirt, she pulls his elbow through the sleeve. They struggle a bit and she notes that Peter has his eyes and interest centered on his elbow.

"That's your elbow, Peter," she says. "See my elbow . . . can you say elbow?"

They feel each other's elbow and Peter repeats after her several times. His interest soon shifts and Mary does not press him further. But she will remember to come back to that word several times in the future until Peter remembers it. In this way Mary is steadily building Peter's vocabulary through use of their daily activities together.

As they go back to the bedroom, Mary points out the colors in his articles of clothing. She remembers what colors he learned last week and repeats quickly in passing on to new words. She very casually reviews what he has already learned and adds a new color to the list. Future repetition and review will make the new color a permanent part of Peter's vocabulary.

As Peter and Mary prepare for breakfast, his mind is exposed to number ideas as they count the spoons as they are placed on the table. Mary is careful to move along quickly so that Peter will not lose interest. She knows that many opportunities will come during the week. She does not need to press hard for instant mastery. She knows that she can repeat tomorrow and all week long. No need to be "uptight" or "pushy" with Peter. Her method is relaxed and easy. She adds to Peter's arithmetic skill every day, but she does it only in the natural setting of the day's activities. There is absolutely no pressure. She looks for a time when interest is high. There is no need to hurry. She has weeks and months to teach. Her incidental method will be filled with hundreds of opportunities to repeat an idea tomorrow, next week, and next month. Her purpose is to stimulate the child's mind, to nurture steady progress, to praise him with each major milestone of achievement, and to build self-confidence.

Following breakfast Peter and his mother are off to the supermarket. They go twice each week to buy groceries. Mary uses the trips to the market as a rich teaching and learning experience for Peter. She tries to review what he has learned and to detect concepts that have been forgotten. They look for colors, numbers, rectangles, triangles, and squares. They learn about big, bigger, and biggest as they select boxes of cereal. With Peter sitting in the front of the shopping cart, they whiz up and down the aisles with a constant conversation flowing between them. Mary looks for neighbors and store employees who are acquainted with Peter. She wants to expand his social skills by exposing him to many types of people and to varying personalities. The supermarket is one of her teaching laboratories. She applies the incidental teaching method here by watching for high interest responses from Peter. She is thinking about her grocery shopping and Peter's incidental learning experiences at the same time.

Since it is Monday afternoon, Peter and his mother know that it is time to go to the basement to do the laundry. Mary uses Peter to help sort items of clothing; they put white and colored items in separate piles. Peter helps to get socks that match and to do other things that will keep him active and involved.

Mary knows that Peter is learning his new words from her. She knows that she must pronounce her words correctly. She knows that her attitude and her mood will influence Peter. She tries to be positive and cheerful even if the days seem a bit dreary and discouraging.

That evening Mary and her husband discuss Peter's vocabulary. They try to remember all the words that he knows and they plan between them to expand his use of the language because they know that this will nurture his mind, keep him alert and communicative. They share ideas and plans for future incidental learning lessons. They talk about Peter's growing mind and its care and feeding with the same concern that they have for his growing body and its nutrition. They have a plan for teaching him, but they will execute that plan only as it seems natural to do so through incidental teaching.

From the foregoing discussion you should understand the simple concept of incidental teaching as practiced in the home. This is in contrast to the formal method where parents sit down and try to conduct a school-type teaching session. The latter is usually not very successful, but the former is almost a sure winner if parents are willing to think education and apply the incidental teaching method in a consistent and continuous effort over the preschool and regular school years. The incidental teaching process begins at age four months as the parents equip the baby's crib with bright colors, mobiles, and mind-stimulating sounds and movements. The process ends as the youth leaves home for college and a subsequent life of adult independence.

The content of the incidental teaching process grows with the child. In the fourth grade, for example, the parents are actively concerned about the school curriculum. They browse through the science, social studies, mathematics, and English textbooks. They talk about current events and history related to the social studies program at school. They think of the applied science principles around the home. They look for times to teach fractions, the multiplication tables, and other mathematics concepts. They apply the same principles that were discussed in the typical day in the life of three-year-old Peter and his mother, but they adjust the level to challenge a fourth grader. By the fourth grade, the child's special interests and talents are unfolding. The needs and shortcomings are known. Through the active concern of the parents, the fourth grade child's mind is constantly stimulated to apply in the outside world what is learned at school and at home. But this is done incidentally and comes out of the regular events and natural circumstances as the parent and the fourth grader work and live together.

The supermarket experience will be continued as part of the incidental teaching process. But the learning dialogue will be on a different level from that of Peter and his mother. The parent and the fourth grader will discuss the best buys, the discounts, the grades of meat and produce, and so forth.

The experiences at home will center more on conserving energy, on detergents that will be environmentally harmless, on gas versus electric clothes dryers, and on automobile operation and maintenance that will conserve fuel and save money. *But the conversation will continue to flow in the home where parents are active and where they enjoy the interaction with the minds of their children as they employ the techniques of incidental teaching.* Following is another example:

Tom Jones is the father of Susan, aged twelve. He picks up his daughter every Tuesday at approximately 5:20 P.M., outside the entrance to a private music school where Susan is studying piano. Tom noticed one Tuesday that Susan was very quiet, short in answers to questions.

As they drove along the boulevard toward home, Tom

finally persuaded Susan to talk about her worries. It turned out that Susan had failed a test in math, had been singled out before the entire class as an example of a student who could do better but was just lazy.

"The plain truth is, Dad, I don't like math. I get all uptight and can't even remember my own name when we get into math," Susan complained. "Another thing, I never did really remember my times tables, the way to do long division, and simple stuff like that."

"Susan, I never dreamed you were having these troubles. You've always been at least a B student in school," Tom replied to his daughter. "Let's talk about it more. Maybe I can help you while we make the long drive home every Tuesday."

"It will take more than that!" Susan responded tearfully.

"I was always pretty good at math," Tom replied. "We can think of ways to help. Math can really be fun. It is mostly simple logic, and a bright young lady like you can get on to it."

This conversation started Tom Jones in a new role as Susan's special mentor for all her studies. Tom established a special rapport with Susan that had never existed before. He soon learned to talk about other matters related to her social life, boy-girl problems, and the entire realm of concern in the life of a twelve-year-old daughter.

The conversations on Tuesdays following Susan's weekly piano lesson became a source of special joy to her. She looked forward to the long ride home in the heavy, 5:30 P.M. traffic, and she saved certain problems for discussion with her father.

Tom used the front seat of the family car as a special tutorial for Susan. From his early conversations he quickly learned of the extent of Susan's mathematics deficiencies. He soon found that his mind was often searching—almost subconsciously—for ways to explain special math concepts to Susan. They devised a special game, for example, using the first digit to appear on a license plate before them. They would multiply this by the second digit as a means of stimulating Susan to master a fundamental skill that she failed to develop in earlier years. She was also exposed to the logic behind some fundamental math processes as Tom used the incidents of their ride home as an opportunity to lend encouragement and offer opportunities to do some drill on math skills.

Tom discussed Susan's problems in mathematics with her mother. They planned together to help Susan. Tom found other opportunities to help Susan gain both confidence and competence in mathematics as they shared experiences around the home and neighborhood. For example, Tom shared with Susan his concerns about automobile operating expenses such as mileage, depreciation, when to trade in on a new car, and so on. As Susan and her father shared these matters that were of concern to Tom, it soon emerged as a natural outcome to apply the mathematical implications. On the Tuesday drive home it was impossible for Tom to do computations on paper. He used this as an excuse to get Susan to figure gas mileage, tire discounts, and to apply math to the conversation about the family car. Tom learned to slip in a few math lessons incidentally when the conversation was on the family grocery bill, the coming costs of sending Susan to college, as well as in the discussion of the immediate circumstances of operating the family automobile. Tom soon learned that he could help Susan to gain confidence in math by helping her to think of real life, family-related problems where mathematics skill was required.

Susan discussed her fear of tests and examinations at school. Tom helped his daughter to learn how to take tests by learning more about them himself from a visit to the junior high school. They discussed the need to prepare for exams. Tom learned about the schedule for term examinations. He would then help Susan to review as they sat together in the front seat of their car. Following the exam, they would talk about the results, go over the test itself, and quietly analyze the mistakes.

These incidental learning experiences led to both an intellectual and psychological closeness between father and daughter. Tom, from many conversations, gained a fairly good inventory of Susan's academic strengths and weaknesses. He would then look for incidents where he could apply a real life situation to a teaching opportunity with Susan:

"I need to get some new snow tires, Susan. Why don't you look through the ads in the paper and see where we might get the best buy?"

"Do you need white walls or black?" Susan asked.

"I don't know. White walls look better. But are they worth it?" Susan's father responded.

"It looks to me like they cost about $4.00 per tire more for white walls," Susan said.

"What percent increase is that?" Tom inquired.

This led to a chance to discuss the problem, with Susan using her school notebook, her father leading the incidental lesson.

"You have to pay a federal excise tax, Dad. What's that

and why do we have it?" Susan inquired after the black wall versus white wall problem had been solved.

"That's how we pay for this freeway we are driving on right now, Susan." Tom explained.

This led to a discussion of the excise tax and how it was calculated on the tires they were about to buy. But they also moved into a civics lesson on federal taxes and the federal freeway system. This in turn led to a discussion of public versus private transportation, about the nation's fuel and energy problems and the question as to whether the government should regulate private automobile travel during rush hour traffic like the situation they were in at that very moment.

Tom had learned a bit about Susan's social studies classwork at school. He used this opportunity to discuss freedom and government regulation—the problems of controlling personal liberties for the common good of all and the problems of too much control. He used this conversation to stimulate Susan's thoughts and to draw her thinking into an understanding of the problems faced by lawmakers and other officials in government.

As Susan and her father passed an intersection where freeway construction had been stopped for the past year, Tom had an opportunity to explain to Susan about a big lawsuit that was before the federal courts concerning the route of the freeway through a section of a huge parkway. Tom was able to explain the process for settling disputes and the rights of citizen groups to sue the government and gain a hearing and a decision. This conversation was renewed each Tuesday as they would drive by the site where the freeway construction was stopped. As the lawsuit came to trial before the court, Tom would ask Susan to read the account of the trial from the newspaper. He would then use this occasion for more incidental teaching about the three branches of government and how they functioned.

From these experiences that Tom shared with his daughter, he soon became deeply interested in her school life and in her intellectual growth and social development. He took every opportunity that came along to teach Susan and stimulate her to think rationally and objectively. His teaching grew out of the natural experiences that they shared. He avoided assuming command over Susan's learning and never attempted to "hold school" at home in a formal setting. His approach was casual, low key, and one of utilization of precious teaching moments when interest was high and the circumstance was natural and relaxed. Susan learned to overcome her almost irrational fear of mathematics. She also gained a great amount of information about many other subjects. Her father functioned as a teacher but she was never aware of it. They just seemed to share their problems with each other and to be close friends. Susan learned to relieve her fears and worries by using her father as a counselor and an outlet for her apprehensions. Tom planned each week to help Susan. He knew her needs as well as her wants and desires. He helped to lead her mind away from petty concerns to more mature thinking. He enjoyed his new role and looked forward to each Tuesday and their ride home. The Tuesday rides led to other occasions in the week when they would share experiences. Each incident seemed to lead to another as Tom took over in carrying out his role as a father and incidental teacher of his daughter.

The foregoing example of incidental teaching offers very little that is new and revolutionary in the teaching and learning process. But it does point out the opportunities available that are ignored either from neglect or from a lack of readiness on the part of parents to turn incidental experiences into learning opportunities. Many parents would use a weekly automobile ride on the freeway for almost anything but an educational program. *Too many parents fail to think about education as their responsibility. They permit those hours of constant contact with their children to pass by without turning them to the benefit of learning and intellectual growth.*

Following are seven basic points to remember about incidental teaching and how to apply it in your home:

1. *Incidental teaching begins with active parent concern for nurturing the minds of their children.* Parents must recognize that they are the most influential of all teachers. You must think education, and your role as a teacher, as being critical to your total responsibility as a parent. *You must, first of all, be an actively concerned parent.*

2. *Remember that conversation teaches.* You must have meaningful communication if you are to be effective in employing the incidental method of home-based instruction. This conversation must be a two-way flow of thoughts and ideas. Get your child to talk openly and freely. This is the key to information for you. Without this you cannot be successful.

3. *Learn about what is on your child's mind.* Learn about his or her aches, fears, hopes, desires, interests, attitudes, strengths, and weaknesses. Do this by developing your listening skills. Do this by not being domineering and by leading your child into special trust and complete confidence that you are a friend as well as a parent.

4. *Know about the content of the school curriculum in which your child is currently engaged.* Ask your child to bring his or her textbooks home. Review the table of contents. Become familiar with the level of study skills being taught at school and keep current through:
    a. review of tests and papers that come home;
    b. review of the current chapters in the textbooks; and
    c. keeping in touch with the teacher by availing yourself of every opportunity for a conference, a casual chat, or a telephone conversation.

5. *Execute your incidental teaching plans every day as new experiences unfold.* Watch for levels of high interest that will suggest that you have a special incident in your child's life that is a teaching opportunity. In the execution of your plans be sure that you are not a "pushy," domineering parent. You cannot be a successful teacher employing the incidental method if you let yourself take over, "hold school," and demand responses. Your approach must be very casual. But it must be part of an overall goal. You must recognize that your teaching is individualized and designed for one person. You will have hundreds of opportunities in a single month. Have clearly fixed in your mind those learning outcomes you want to help your child achieve and then reach them casually, systematically, and very gradually as an outgrowth of life's ongoing experiences with your child. Your incidental teaching process is a way of living with your child as much as it is a methodology. If you think of learning needs and if you think constantly of ways to use daily incidents as teaching and learning occasions, the entire approach will soon become second nature to you. Your child will soon be learning without being conscious of the fact that he or she is mastering new skills and gaining added knowledge.

6. *The skill of questioning is as important as listening when you use the incidental teaching method.* Artful questioning

will stimulate your child's mind. It will touch off more questions and further conversation. Make sure that your questions help to build rapport and enhance the interaction with your child's mind. Questioning is, of course, a two-way process in the casual setting of incidental teaching. Often a teaching episode will be touched off by your child's question. As you reply, make sure that you answer fully but not at such length as to discourage other questions. If you respond appropriately to the questions and gain understanding through your own inquiries, you will carry out a process that will motivate your child to want to learn more. After an incidental teaching session be sure to review what happened. Try to determine if a few well-placed questions would have added to the productiveness of your exchange.

7. *Make each week a learning cycle*. *Plan* what you will teach during the coming week. *Implement* your plan through the incidental method as you proceed with your regular weekly routine. *Evaluate* the results of your child's learning as the week unfolds. *Revise* your plans as a result of new information growing out of the week's activities. Think of the word, *PIER* as a guide to each weekly cycle of incidental teaching. *Plan, implement, evaluate,* and *revise* as you go through each week's experience with your child. In doing this you will turn life itself into a learning experience for your child as you come to realize that all experience teaches all of us throughout all of our days.

HOW TO "MAKE" A CURRICULUM IN THE HOME

We will now turn our attention to further elaboration of what to teach at home. From this discussion you should understand more about how to "make" a curriculum at home. In order to do this you should consider closely what the objectives of your child's education should cover—what capacities, knowledge, and personal attributes we are seeking.

THE OBJECTIVES AND PURPOSES OF EDUCATION

What should be the purposes of education? Knowing that a child cannot learn everything, what learning is of the most worth? Conversely, are we teaching concepts at home that are of little value?

What should be our learning priorities? After a list of learning outcomes or objectives has been established, what should come first and what should be last?

As you begin to think in terms of a home-based curriculum for your children, you need to think about objectives. You need to consider thoughtfully those things that you think your children should learn, and thus establish priorities. A brief discussion of educational objectives and learning priorities might be useful as a prelude to further discussion of the home-based curriculum. Following are nine broad objectives that should guide your thinking as you develop your own home-based curriculum:

1. It is trite but true to emphasize that education should help a child develop his or her talents. Good education should lead children to develop fundamental study skills. The basic subject matter essential to further learning should be taught in the public schools. Graduates from our public schools should be able to read, write, use basic mathematics, and have a fundamental background necessary for a period of lifelong learning.

2. Since we live in a democratic society, it is argued convincingly that a major purpose of education should be to foster and develop democracy as a way of life. Children should be taught how to carry out the important responsibilities of citizenship in a democracy. It is further argued that attitudes and appreciations are essential. Therefore, we should not neglect these vital aspects of learning.

3. Good health is essential for true fulfillment in life. Therefore, instruction in the fields of health and physical education is deemed essential in considering the curriculum. Any program of home-based instruction should not neglect this vital area. Since most of the living takes place in the home, perhaps the home carries a heavier responsibility for health and physical education than does the school. Certainly both physical and mental health should be worthy outcomes sought by parents deeply involved in helping to educate their children.

4. Vocational and career education are important. Both the home and the school should thoughtfully develop the child's talents so that the individual can participate in our free economic system on a level that will bring about self-sufficiency and a

positive contribution to the economic strength of the home, community, state, and nation. Helping children to make wise choices in planning for a career and in utilizing education to achieve the utmost in career development must be a high priority. Many critics of the school argue that this very practical aspect of education is neglected and that too much favor is given to the abstract academic subjects. The academicians argue that the key to true career success lies in mastery of the academics, that academic education is, in fact, universal career education. Regardless of where the emphasis should be, parents must become more knowledgeable and must assume more responsibility for career education. The home and the school must do much more to form a solid working relationship in this very vital aspect of education.

5. Education for future parental responsibilities is emphasized as a vital aspect of teaching and learning activity. Advocates of more emphasis in this area point to the number of broken homes and to the recent trends toward deterioration in the quality of home life as evidence that we need to teach young people more about their future parental responsibilities.

6. As we consider the human attributes that we want our children to possess, we certainly cannot overlook character development. We want our children, as future adults, to become strongly committed to high ideals and to have the capacity of self-discipline. A strong will, ability to discipline oneself and to work conscientiously for some high-level goals must be considered in any profile of highly desirable human attributes. The ability to face adversity and to overcome difficulties is important to a successful life. All of this is considered under the heading of character education. Many would also include the attributes of honesty, sincerity, and compassion under this heading. These outcomes are hard to teach but they are considered essential. The teaching of religious concepts and adherence to high spiritual ideals must be a prime responsibility of the home. Needless to say, the school should not neglect the entire realm of spiritual, moral, and character development. Many thoughtful leaders in education believe that the entire realm of character education must begin with religious instruction. This aspect must, of course, be reserved for the home and church.

7. If students are to learn to enjoy a life of participation

in neighborhood and community events, they must have certain social skills and capacities. The child must learn to be comfortable in a group and to be able to enjoy participating in the dynamics of social organizations. It is believed that such social skills will lead to active citizenship and the realization of full responsibility in a democratic society where the citizens must make decisions. Social understanding, social activity, and social justice are all emphasized as vital outcomes that must be taught at home and at school as we strive to educate the whole child.

8. Economic efficiency and how to apply the so-called scientific method to living would be included in a list of objectives by many educators. One needs a certain level of economic literacy in a free enterprise system. Where credit is easy to get and debt equally easy to acquire, it is essential that young people learn how to manage money and how to become an efficient part of our economic system. Although this area may be closely connected with career and occupational education, personal economics and solid consumer judgment must be taught in the home and at school if our youth are to become wise, productive, and self-fulfilling citizens.

9. The esthetic aspects of living should be taught at home and at school. A rich and meaningful life cannot be attained without some appreciation of the arts and humanities. Love and appreciation of fine music, art, drama, and great literature must be a worthy educational objective. Emphasis in the arts and humanities must not be neglected as we think of the curriculum at home and at school. We must plan for experiences that will develop a rich life with deep meaning surrounded by the beauties of life in this modern age.

THE HOME-BASED CURRICULUM

The first point to remember in building your own home-based curriculum is that you must enrich the school program and not function in competition or in opposition to it. For this reason you should pay particular attention to point number four under "Basic points to remember about incidental teaching and how to apply it in your home" (see page 43). You should follow what is being taught at school by keeping in touch with the school program.

Suggestions for enrichment of the regular school program will be found in subsequent pages where the school curriculum is discussed in further detail. As you employ your own incidental teaching method, the school curriculum should be one of the important guides for the subject matter content you will emphasize at home.

Following are some aspects of learning outcomes and objectives that need special emphasis in your home-based curriculum, for these are areas where you must assume a heavy responsibility:*

1. *Effective and Accurate Use of the Language.*

Language is the tool used by your children to acquire all their knowledge. Children learn the language from their parents. They learn to speak, listen, and communicate in the home. You teach your children their first vocabulary—for good or ill. You will have a more powerful influence on your child's language, vocabulary, speaking habits, and speech mannerisms than anyone else. This is the first and foremost item in your home-based curriculum.

Of the entire educational process, the use of the mother tongue is the most important factor. All the great wisdom of the ages is stored with the printed words of the language. Language will build your child's mental processes, discipline the mind, and provide the keys to all that will subsequently be learned.

Since language is the key to knowledge acquisition, you must remember that almost everything depends upon how well you teach your child to use this tool. Speak correctly and distinctly. Use proper grammar and use words that are clearly understood. Constantly expand you child's vocabulary. Teach a love for words and a curiosity for their meaning.

Be sure to correct defects in speech. Don't laugh at mistakes or encourage errors of speech by thinking that it is childlike and cute to make errors. Don't encourage baby talk by repeating it. Remember that language teaching is a prime home responsibility.

You will help solve future problems of spelling, learning to read, and pronunciation if you do a creditable job of teaching the mother tongue to your child. Moreover, if you fail in this task—if you miseducate by your poor example—your child will have handicaps to overcome.

---

*For further information on a home-based curriculum you may want to read Thomas W. Evans, *The School in the Home* (New York: Harper and Row, 1973), chapter 3.

Speak to your child in well-enunciated syllables so that the ears hear words distinctly and the child hears all the parts of a word pronounced as it should be. Listen to your child and repeat the proper pronunciation but do not inhibit speech by aggressive interference. Your example, more than anything else, will teach the mother tongue to your child. This requires that you help your child through your own use of the language.

Since there is no tool subject in the curriculum that will clarify thought, discipline the mind, and motivate further desire to learn as much as effective and easy use of the language, you must build power and capacity in your child from the beginning. Teach new words, their meaning and proper use, every week as you pursue your incidental teaching plans. As you follow the PIER cycle each week (plan, implement, evaluate, and revise), *be sure to build vocabulary and expand it constantly.* This is a continuous challenge and one that you will enjoy if you pursue it in your planning and execution of your teaching responsibilities.

Remember that: (a) language power has its beginning in the home; (b) the foremost problem of education is to create first in the minds of children a rich and varied knowledge of the language and the thousands of words that comprise it; and (c) all thinking is in terms of language, and the power to think and learn is language-based. Therefore, your home-based curriculum must begin with effective teaching of the language.

2. *Mastery and Confidence in Mathematics.*

In the school situation, mathematics is a subject that children seem to learn either to detest or to adore. Unfortunately, far too many children develop an intense dislike for mathematics. Many establish a deep-seated mental aversion to anything involving numbers and mathematical reasoning. As a parent, you may have some of these attitudinal and emotional responses. But children should learn to think numerically and mathematically in the home. If you start early and help your children to have fun with numbers, they will develop a love for this subject that will be of great value to them all their lives.

It has been said that mathematics is the "language" of science. Surely, in the early years of your child's life it will be easy for you to teach number concepts through the incidental method as you work and play together in the home. In the process you will be teaching language and adding to the power of the child's vocabulary.

Your home-based curriculum should include an awareness of numbers and their meaning. You begin with counting spoons, saucers, and napkins as you prepare the table for meals. You move on in the incidental process by *demonstrating* with specific items how subtraction and addition works. (Place items on the floor and show the meaning of five spoons and two spoons to equal seven. Teach subtraction in the same way in the laundry as you count stockings. Teach numbers in the supermarket as you count the carrots and oranges.)

The home-based mathematics curriculum should extend gradually as the child grows intellectually. The recipes in cooking, the miles per gallon in the automobile, the interest on the home mortgage payments, the sales tax at the store—all of these are opportunities to apply the incidental teaching process for alert parents who are practicing active concern for their child's education.

If children grow up using mathematics concepts in their daily lives they will not fear math instruction at school and they will have developed in their natural living circumstances the cognitive power to master the challenges of mathematics. Your child can learn the basics of arithmetic very early in the home if you are both alert and consistent in teaching addition, subtraction, multiplication, division, fractions, and percentages.

Arithmetic is a very easy subject to teach through use of the incidental technique. Fractions, for example, can be taught in the kitchen as portions of food are allocated among the family members. All that is required is a willingness to interact with your child, stimulate the intellect, and gradually build one arithmetic skill after another. A little thought and planning each week will produce unlimited learning opportunities.

3. *The Scientific Method and Capacity for Objective Thinking.*

In your home-based teaching practices and in your daily conversation with your child you must give a high priority to building a capacity to think objectively and to use logic in approaching problems. Stimulate your child's mind to look for evidence to support conclusions and decisions. Teach your child to look beyond the lavish and often unfounded claims of politicians, commercial advertising, and the like. This ability will largely be shaped by what the child hears and observes from parents.

You should encourage your child to seek varied opinions,

to consult more than one source, and quietly and thoughtfully to weigh the best evidence in making decisions. In making important purchases for the home the child may learn a decision-making process of great value if you apply the best logic and careful thought in arriving at major buying decisions. Be sure to include your child in the conversation.

All of our homes are filled with the marvels of applied science. Our residences consume energy, utilize chemicals, and apply certain principles of life science. Everything from selecting and applying lawn fertilizer to sterilizing a thermometer before taking a child's temperature will afford opportunities to teach application of scientific principles and demonstrate the value of objective thinking. Children are particularly interested in plants and animals. Pets and home gardening projects provide numerous opportunities for incidental lessons in science.

4. *The Social Sciences and the Principles of Humane Living.*

In your home the responsibilities of the "office of citizen" should be taught to your children. Each child should grow up with an awareness that active civic responsibility is the price that we pay for freedom.

Plan your home-based teaching activities to include continuous exposure to the basic concepts of government and the way our free enterprise system functions. Read and discuss newspapers, editorials, weekly news magazines. Watch television newscasts, documentaries, and special features with your children. Provide opportunities for attendance at meetings of city councils, county commissions, sessions of the legislature, and special hearings and civic gatherings.

The home atmosphere must be one of awareness, concern, and participation in building a better America, a better state, a better city, and a better neighborhood; and the home-based curriculum should focus upon this enormous and pressing need.

Parents should be thoughtfully concerned about prejudice and how it can be learned. Children in the home should hear the voice of tolerance, moderation, and respect for ethnic and racial minorities. Children should have parent-sponsored experiences whereby they can be involved in civic projects and can participate in discussions and debates that constitute major decisions in the making. Only through living democracy and through experiencing the dynamics of government in action will children truly become citizen participants in the real sense.

The home-based curriculum must include an awareness of the need for economic education. Too many parents avoid discussing the realities of income and outgo and family finances. Through family living children should learn to handle money wisely and to gain a real sense of involvement in the economic system. Experience in the home should teach the child the advantages and perils of debt, in a society where credit is easy and indebtedness can be incurred to a burdensome extent. The dynamics of home and family life should teach the great virtue of thrift. As parents consider the social studies curriculum at home, they must be introspective about what family finances are teaching the child about economics and his or her own personal involvement in family economics. Many parents neglect this heavy responsibility. The home-based curriculum must recognize the fact that economic education is going on either directly or indirectly every month of the child's life.

In considering the social studies curriculum, parents must resolve to be, first of all, excellent living examples of good citizenship. The economics of home and family living must be taught through exemplary action. The right, the need, and the responsibility for participation in community and governmental affairs can be taught more dramatically by parental example than by any other means.

Another aspect of home-based teaching is demonstrating the value of certain civic improvement projects in the community. Get your children involved in charitable drives that assist the less fortunate. Have them join you in civic club projects to improve community facilities such as parks, swimming pools, and so on.

Many parents make a serious error in excluding children from some of the serious problems, issues, and even scandalous events that occur in a community. Children old enough to understand should be brought into the real life of the family, neighborhood, and community. The conversation that centers on local issues will be stimulating and mind stretching to older children and youth. Plan your social science teaching at home out of daily events which your child will become aware of as soon as he or she is old enough to learn from such experiences. This will stimulate interests that can be utilized to encourage reading, vocabulary, and many other aspects of your total program of home-based teaching.

5. *Music, Art, and Literature.*

These subjects refine the soul and provide depth and

meaning to living. Your children should grow up in a home surrounded with fine artwork and other objects of beauty.

Your children will have criteria for quality in music if they experience at home the opportunity to hear the classics as well as modern music of high quality.

Be sure to involve your child in the selection of paintings and other works of art that you choose for your home. Give your child an opportunity to decorate his or her own room and to have a sense of identity and ownership of items of beauty. The same applies to selection of records and tapes for your home music library.

Books and periodicals of high quality should be available in your home. Don't miss the pleasure of reading some of the great classics of literature to your child. Encourage reading and discuss with your child your own reading interests.* The incidental teaching method can be used to great benefit as you discuss the characters and the plots of some of the well-known novels, short stories, and plays. Such discussion will enrich your conversation and provide you with opportunities for incidental teaching as you share experiences through the art, music, and literature in your home.

Children eager to participate in school music programs where some mastery of a musical instrument is necessary will need to have some private lessons and will require encouragement and support for constant practice at home. Children who display an interest in and talent for expressing feelings on paper through sketching or painting should receive encouragement and should have an opportunity through the home to develop this special skill. The modern school curriculum offers specialized instruction that can be a great asset to parents, but the full realization of one's interests and abilities must come out of the intimate contact of the home. This is not to say that some great and distinguished artists and musicians have not risen from the sadness of a totally nonsupportive home. However, such outcomes are very rare and occur in spite of the home rather than because of it. As a parent, be very sensitive to the expressive tendencies of your children in art, music, and literature.

Some parents insist on making a concert pianist or a ballet dancer out of a child who lacks interest and whose talents may lie

---

*Nancy Larrick's book, *A Parent's Guide to Children's Reading* (New York: Doubleday, Inc., 1969), is one of the most authoritative sources for selecting children's literature.

in another direction. It takes great compassion and parental insight to distinguish between the responsibility of teaching appreciation of the arts and building in depth upon a child's special talent and interest. You should be realistic in your aspirations for your children. You must have the firmness to encourage your child to practice enough to develop special talents, yet not overdo it to the point where pressure causes emotional problems that will have a negative impact upon the child. Give music, art, and literature the support and attention that they merit without generating negative attitudes and emotional responses that are counterproductive.

An important fact to keep in mind is that the early years will provide your greatest opportunity to guide your child and cultivate talent in music and art. Those early years seem to shape the inclinations and discipline the will to express in music and art the inherent talents. Begin your efforts early and be sure to include stimulation for the arts in your incidental teaching.

6. *Health and Physical Activity.*

You should strive to nurture a physically active child. Sponsor opportunities for learning individual sports such as swimming, golf, and tennis. If a degree of mastery and skill are achieved in the early years, your child will be inclined to enjoy sports throughout the later years and into adult life. In leading your child into a well-rounded life, do not neglect teaching a life pattern that will help to build a strong body.

Encourage participation in team sports and see that your child benefits from group activity in the neighborhood, community, and at school.

In your incidental teaching help your child to understand the basics in sound health practice. Teach and practice good nutrition. See that your child cares for his or her body from the beginning of life and the rewards will continue to be realized for years.

7. *Social Competence.*

Your child must learn how to get along with others—to make friends and to be a friend. It is hard for the school to teach this on an individualized basis. For a child to develop in this area of competence, most of the assistance and guidance must come from home, with a lesser amount of help from the school, neighborhood, church, and community.

Most children develop their social skills by trial and error as they relate to their peers. But all too often parents begin too late in the child's life. They must try to sponsor conditions where social competence is learned at home, and they must offer guidance and constant encouragement. You should encourage your children to have friends in your home. By hosting parties and other activities at home your child will learn to be poised and confident in social activity with others. The least that you can do is to provide the setting and be available for suggestions.

If you encourage a child to be self-centered because of your behavior toward him or her, the child will find life difficult and a bit cruel outside of your home. Your child must learn to give and take at home as well as on the playground and in the neighborhood. Teach your child to share and to be socially considerate.

Your incidental teaching activity will make a powerful contribution to this essential skill if you are actively concerned. Observe your child's social growth and provide the stimulation and learning opportunities.

8. *Ambition, Drive, Character, and Will.*

Educators are frank to admit that they do not know how to teach these attributes in school. These qualities of ambition, will to succeed, and tenaciousness of purpose are vital. Perhaps more important than innate talent and inherited intelligence is the *will to achieve*. You should strive to foster these qualities in your child. Success seems to be contagious. If you establish conditions wherein your child can be successful, and if you offer reward and recognition for genuine effort and objectively measured accomplishment, you will have taken a big step in building your own home-based program of character development.

In your incidental teaching program, help your child experience the joy of accomplishment. Do this by presenting challenges and helping to create conditions that will enhance the probability of success. If you are close to your child and if you get a "feel" for his or her needs for challenge and meaningful endeavor, you will know almost intuitively the means of offering motivation, work assignment, and recognition for accomplishment.

One of the great lessons that your child should learn from you is the will to do what ought to be done when it should be done—whether one wants to do it or not. This discipline of the will and cultivation of ambition and drive to accomplishment comes through a long process. In your incidental teaching you should:

    a. talk to your child about the qualities of character needed to be successful;
    b. teach about the joys of accomplishment and the genuine pleasure of work;
    c. help your child to finish successfully tasks that are assigned, and make regular assignments that are within the child's ability but sufficiently challenging;
    d. gradually lead your child to independence and self-reliance by encouraging and helping but also by studiously avoiding doing for your child what he or she is capable of doing;
    e. make sure that your child's work efforts are successful most of the time so that the ego is not damaged;
    f. see that there are motivation, recognition, and rewards for accomplishment of meaningful work in your home;
    g. be consistent and avoid capriciousness in your work assignments and enforcement of them; and
    h. see that your child has his or her own possessions and personal property and that these are under the child's exclusive control and full ownership. (Note: The ownership of one's own "wealth"—regardless of its value to others—is important in motivation and character building. Your child should have his or her own private place in the home and a sacred place where possessions can be kept. By learning to have and hold the fruits of his or her labor, your child will learn early in life about the pleasure of "owning" property and acquiring things of value. This should be a central concept in your thinking about character development and inculcation of ambition and drive in your child's total personality.)

As you conclude this chapter on the incidental teaching method and the home-based curriculum you should have a basic understanding of: (1) how to teach in the natural setting of your home as you go about working, playing, living, and sharing with your children; and (2) what to teach and what knowledge, skills, attitudes, and personality qualities you want to instill into the mind and basic character of your children. Remember that you must be constantly concerned and actively committed to the home-based learning of your child. Apply the principles of incidental teaching every week and strive to follow the PIER (plan, implement, evaluate, and revise) cycle of weekly application of this method. Strive to be an actively concerned parent and you will reap the richest rewards of parenthood.

4.
What You Should Know About Your Child's School

In this chapter you will learn about how schools function. You will get an inside view of the school and its problems. You will learn about the school day and scheduling of students in the school curriculum. Suggestions will be given as to how you might get to know your child's teachers and how you might cooperate with the school to help attain the greatest results for your child. Responding to reports and calls from the school and knowing when to intervene in problems that your child is having and when to let your child fight his or her own battles and solve his or her own problems will also be discussed. From this chapter you should gain insight into the problems of schools and more practical knowledge about specific ways that you can relate to your child's school in offering support to your child and to the school.

THE SCHOOL DAY

Schools must be operated on a regular basis by the clock and by the calendar. You should understand the school day and the daily schedule of the child. Many parents add to the burdens of teachers by permitting and even encouraging children to be late for school. Children must learn early in life that regular attendance and prompt compliance with the school schedule are important responsibilities. Your activities in the home should reflect this concern and lend positive support.

From time to time it is necessary to take a child from school in order to keep a dental or medical appointment. If you understand the school schedule and recognize the times in the day when heavy teaching activities are planned, you can avoid taking your child out of school at the most crucial time. Some parents totally ignore the school schedule and the school calendar in making decisions to take a child out of school. It is important for a child to be present for term examinations, for the introductory teaching of a new unit in a solid subject area, and at other times when the child has a specific responsibility. As a parent you should be familiar with your child's daily routine. Let your decisions be sensitive to this routine so that your plans can minimize the amount of interruption.

RESPONDING TO REPORTS AND CALLS FROM SCHOOL

Most schools strive to keep in close contact with parents. They want to describe the school curriculum. They may want to communicate with you on a special problem involving your child. You should respond to these communications and keep in constant touch with the school.

The most traditional and time-honored method of reporting from school to home is, of course, the report card. You should pay close attention to the report card that your child brings home. Make sure that you understand the card. Read the instructions and the interpretations printed on it. Also, be sure to call your child's teacher if there are aspects of the card that need clarification. You need to understand the reporting system and how the teacher uses the system if you are going to have a good understanding of the progress your child is making in school. Be sure to discuss the report card with your child and also follow up on any question that you might have by getting in touch with the teacher. If you expect the teacher to have an intense interest in the education of your child, you must, of course, display such interest yourself. Use the report card as a means of establishing regular communication.

Many parents—even the experienced and well educated—fail to use the report card to their child's full benefit. It is surprising to learn how little parent attention is paid to the total information on a school report card. There is more to be learned than academic progress and relative standing in the class. Many school systems give some evaluation of the child's social maturity. Promptness in doing work, ability to get along with others, participation in activities other than academics are all factors in your child's school performance that may be more important than academic success.

Most report cards have letter and number codes. They are usually not very complex, but they do require some study on the part of parents. Read every detail on your child's card. Moreover, these details should be discussed in the home. Plans for giving more home-based assistance should be adjusted with each reporting period of the school year.

Parents should follow up with some action after each report card. Parents who fail to contact the school for further information and parents who fail to discuss each child's education progress regularly are not meeting their responsibilities. It takes more than getting the child to school each day to see that he or she is well educated. It requires commitment, constant communication with the school, and diligence to find areas of neglect and decline where special attention and home-based support can be given. Helping your child receive an exceptionally effective education fully commensurate with your child's needs will require your diligent effort. But the time and effort invested are worthwhile on behalf of your child.

Remember that the home must contribute more than moral and financial support to the school. It requires constant attention to many details and steady adjustment to changing needs as the child grows. The school should, of course, pay as much individualized attention to your child as possible, but you have the absolute responsibility to do so. The home is for the individual; it is for fulfilling the self-felt needs and the individual concerns. The personal touch must come from the home so that what is unique to the child will not be missed in the rush of time and in the weight of numbers of children at school. How parents carry out this primary responsibility will largely determine the child's ability to bring all latent talents to full fruition. If you receive nothing more from reading this book than dedication to meet this responsibility, your effectiveness as a parent will be enhanced and your child will benefit greatly.

The report card, special reports, and conferences offered by the school are all laden with opportunity for you to become a more effective parent and for your home to be a more powerful educational influence.

YOUR CHILD'S NEED TO ADAPT AND ADJUST TO THE SCHOOL ENVIRONMENT

The child who gains the capacity to adapt himself or herself to all the problems of school has taken a big step toward learning to cope with the problems of adult life. In many respects the public school is a miniature society in action. In the classroom, in the corridor, and on the playground will be found all types of personalities and a reflection of many human problems. The challenge of adjusting to this school environment is useful to most children.

Avoid entering into the struggles and problems of school life that seem to be part of the learning and adjusting process. The entire purpose of home and school educational activity is, of course, to teach the child to live successfully and happily. Part of this learning is mastering the capacity of fighting one's own battles and working out one's own problems. Except in extreme circumstances where the child cannot solve a problem without help, it is best to allow the youngster to work out his or her own social relationships and to solve interpersonal problems with other children of the same age. This is not to discourage constant interest and ready assistance when needed. But it is to encourage independence, social maturation, and self-reliance.

You should learn to hear both sides of an issue involving your child. This applies to problems related to the teacher and difficulties involving other children. Always remember that it is a natural human tendency to explain a situation in a manner that reflects one favorably. Therefore, stories carried home from school should be considered carefully as one-sided episodes usually described with a naturally biased point of view. In your conversations with your child about school affairs be sure to encourage the youngster to think and tell about both sides of an issue. Constantly raise questions about how the other person might feel in a particular situation. Ask the child to think in terms of the point of view of the teacher. Point out all the problems that the teacher has as the child describes problems and possible deficiencies seen in the teacher. Do the same in matters relating to your child and other children. In these discussions you have a great teaching opportunity if you will stimulate the child to think of the other point of view and to develop the capacity for compassion and empathy. Wise parents can do this while at the same time expressing sympathy and concern for the child's problems. While you are encouraging thought about the point of view of the other person, you can express yourself in a way that assures the child that you are sympathetic and understanding of the problems that are being faced.

One of the greatest advantages of going through a public school system is that an individual can learn how to cope with others. The individual can also learn how to handle competition and pressure. All of this is, of course, useful as children grow gradually into adult life and into the more serious responsibilities of adulthood. Wise parents will look upon these experiences as opportunities for growth. Only when there is a crisis that needs some intervening help should the parents enter into a difficulty at school that involves the child's relationships with others.

GETTING TO KNOW YOUR CHILD'S TEACHER

It is very important that you get to know your child's teacher. Watch for opportunities to do little things that will help the teacher and will show that you appreciate the efforts being made on behalf of your child. Show your sympathy and concern for the great job that the teacher has. But also be very direct in talking about problems that need to be called to the attention of your child's teacher. All this should be done with a solid understanding of the heavy work load carried by the teacher. *Don't let a communications gap exist insofar as the vital problem of educating your child is concerned. Strive to meet the teacher more than halfway in exchanging information and offering suggestions.* But make sure that there is regular communication so your home and the classroom offer mutually supporting activities in accomplishing the serious task of educating your child.

Kathy came home every night complaining that her teacher constantly criticized her before the entire class. She complained of being embarrassed. As the school year moved on, the problem seemed to get worse. At first Kathy's mother ignored her complaints. But it soon became apparent that a crisis was approaching.

When Kathy's mother finally mustered enough courage to call Miss Jones, she was surprised to learn that the teacher had a very serious problem involving Kathy and two close friends. These three girls would divide their assignments, do one-third of the assigned work each, and copy from each other. This cheating led to more cheating on tests. The girls joined each other in a vendetta of negative response to all Miss Jones's efforts.

When Kathy's mother learned that the problem ran deeper than merely one of girls' complaining about a strict teacher, she called the mothers of the other two girls and arranged a conference with the principal and Miss Jones.

The problem was soon diagnosed. After Miss Jones learned that she had the support and confidence of the three girls' mothers, she kept in constant touch. Through close home-school cooperation a major problem was solved. A deep misunderstanding was avoided and closer ties between the school and the homes of the girls were established.

Should you have a feeling that your child's teacher is not very competent, you should be very careful that this attitude does not adversely affect your working relationship. In the eyes of your child, the approach to the teacher must be positive and supportive. This is often very difficult for parents where there are strong feelings toward the teacher. But it is particularly important that these feelings not rub off on the child, for this will add to the problems. Try to work in a positive and constructive way to get at problems you feel need to be corrected. Avoid at all cost creating a feeling of resentment or lack of confidence on the part of the child toward the teacher.

John was a very bright boy. He was also aggressive and outspoken. He would complete his work in class in half the normal time. Then he became restless, caused trouble, and had numerous clashes with his teacher. Instead of challenging John with more work on his level of interest and understanding, his teacher responded to his aggressive behavior with reprisals. He received most of his menial tasks as punishment for his loud behavior.

John had an unusual interest and aptitude in science and mathematics. He displayed no unusual personality problems except for the fact that he was a very self-confident and self-reliant person and might be considered to be a bit conceited.

With 36 students in the room, John's teacher did not have time to get to the bottom of his problem nor to spend extra time with him. Their interpersonal relationship continued to deteriorate. John talked about his teacher and constantly expressed criticism about her at home. John's teacher also complained about him and asked the principal to transfer him to another room.

After worrying about the situation for a long time, John's father and mother finally called the principal to complain; they were convinced that John's troubles stemmed from an incompetent teacher. They asked that John be taken out of her room. The principal reported these calls to John's teacher, and this added to her resentment of John. The clashes became more frequent and the problem attained crisis proportions.

A subsequent meeting in the school district psychologist's office with the teacher and the parents led to another extensive discussion. The psychologist convinced both the teacher and John's parents that he was simply a very bright, aggressive, and self-reliant child who needed constant challenge to his superior and restlessly seeking mind. His school program must be more satisfying and he must be enticed to work on a level that would show him that he had much to learn. He needed more competition to the limit of his ability. The psychologist made suggestions to John's parents as to how they might do more to challenge his abilities at home. He also gave the teacher some sound advice as to how she might use his interest in science to keep him busy and growing intellectually. The meeting with the psychologist resulted in a new school life for John and in a more stimulating home environment. Over a period of three or four months John became good friends with his teacher, and his behavior problems disappeared.

One of the benefits from the foregoing episode was the friendship formed and the means of easy communication opened between school and home. This happened because John's parents finally went to the school and they made use of the school system's special services for problem situations. The teacher and the parents talked through their mutual resentments and frustrations toward each other and settled down to find a joint solution where both the home and school had a role to play.

Too often, parents are reluctant to take the time to do this. Especially where there are problems resulting from strong feelings of criticism, teachers and parents should get together. As a parent, you should do your part to open the discussion and get your concerns before school officials. Remember that some teachers and administrators are also reticent to talk to parents. They instinctively feel that some parents have strong feelings and like to avoid unpleasant confrontations. Make sure that you do not delay solutions to problems at school by your feelings of reluctance to talk about troublesome issues. *Seek complete and frank conversation about problems at school that worry you. By being active in settling complaints that are on your mind, you will be able to put some serious worries behind you.*

TEACHERS AND TEACHING LOADS

Teachers usually receive their work load assignments from the school principal. Teachers with specialties are usually assigned to their areas of greatest competence. Each teacher has a regular schedule to meet and a specific number of students to teach. It is often difficult to assign completely equal numbers of students to each teacher; student numbers vary each year by grade level and by subject matter interest. Therefore, teaching loads are often not exactly equal and some teachers are called upon to carry heavier burdens than others.

The job of the teacher is extremely complex. The state and school district course of study must be taught. A daily schedule is worked out for each school. After this has been done by the principal, each teacher has the responsibility of working out an individual class schedule and a plan for teaching for the year. The great challenge is to utilize the amount of time wisely, to teach the required curriculum effectively, and to meet the individual needs of each student.

In order for equity to be maintained throughout a school system, a formula is usually used to allocate supplies, textbooks, and an instructional budget to each school. The principal, in turn, often allocates materials to each classroom. Standard textbooks adopted by school districts are used. Course of study guides, standardized tests, and other uniform materials and procedures add to the work load and responsibility of the teacher. Each teacher has a record-keeping responsibility. Academic achievement must be noted and recorded. Report cards and attendance reports must be completed. As hallways, playgrounds, lunchrooms, and other areas in the school building and on the grounds must be supervised, each teacher is usually assigned some additional supervisory responsibilities. A teacher may have playground supervising duties one week, hall supervision duties the next week, and lunchroom supervision activity the following week. Faculty members often participate in making decisions on these work load assignments; but after the assignments are made, teachers have burdens to carry in addition to the regular teaching and instruction activities.

One of the biggest problems facing teachers is trying to individualize instruction at the same time that a specific number of students are under the teacher's care. Teachers often struggle with the task of giving individual help to a child who is having a problem mastering a specific skill, while at the same time keeping other students productively busy in the routine of the school day. Pressures from disruptive and unruly students add to this burden. Two or three disruptive students can create an enormous burden on the teacher and can, at the same time, prevent other children in the classroom from having optimum learning opportunities. Parents should be aware of this and should strive to lend support from the home. If you are called about a behavior problem involving your child, you should respond in a very positive way to the plea from the school for assistance. Not only will this be in the best interest of your child, but it will also help other children in the school.

THE PRINCIPAL'S RESPONSIBILITIES

The prime education leader in your neighborhood is, of course, the school principal. In most school systems the principal has broad decision-making authority. The principal must, of course, operate under the rules and regulations of the school district and must comply with state laws regulating schools. But within this framework the principal has considerable authority in making decisions that will affect the day-to-day life of your child. Education-conscious parents should strive to get to know the school principal. If they establish a free and easy working relationship with the principal, telephone conversations can be quickly initiated when problems or misunderstandings emerge. The principal must have the support of the school patrons if a successful educational program is to be sponsored. For this reason, most local school administrators welcome an opportunity to get acquainted with parents and to learn about parental concerns and aspirations.

Most school principals carry an extremely heavy work load. They are responsible for almost everything that goes on inside the school. This includes supervision of the custodial staff, the school lunch workers, the clerical and record-keeping staff, and the teachers and instructional support personnel. In addition to supervising these employees, your school principal will also be busily engaged with the central office personnel in planning curriculum improvements and in implementing new programs and activities that will keep the school educationally up to date. In today's society a large amount of paper work and record-keeping add to the burden of the school principal. Local, state, and federal school forms must be completed regularly as accurate records and reports are made to comply with regulations and with business and academic requirements.

Most school principals strive to develop an educational team that is dedicated to high standards. Regular meetings are held with the faculty. Daily decisions are made concerning the operation of the school building, the caring for school grounds, the administration of the school lunch program, and the execution of the curriculum and the extracurricular activities of the school. Teachers and other school employees having problems demand to spend time in the principal's office, where difficulties are discussed and solutions are worked out. This adds to the daily work load and administrative burden of the school principal. The principal must be an effective leader, a sympathetic person who will listen and respond to problems, and an intelligent individual who is both educational manager, business administrator, and public relations expert.

From the foregoing description of the principal's duties, you can see that the challenges and pressures on a school principal are many. You should keep in mind the broad spectrum of responsibilities of this chief administrative officer and prime school leader for your child's school. Always approach this person with an understanding of these many duties.

If there are problems at school that you believe require the attention of the principal, avoid approaching the principal at a time when there are heavy demands upon his or her time. Immediately before school opens, during the lunch hour, and immediately after school closes most principals are facing many problems and dealing with administrative details. Try to find a time when you can have a conversation that is free from pressure and distractions. The principal's heavy work load, however, should not dissuade you from calling to discuss a problem of serious concern. If the principal's secretary has to take your number and have the principal call back when he or she has time, you should, of course, be understanding of this.

Most parents are too reluctant to call and discuss problems related to school. School administrators generally welcome the opportunity to explain the school program to parents and receive constructive criticism on how matters might be improved.

PARENT VOLUNTEERS

The use of parent volunteers in the modern school is becoming increasingly important. Many parents enjoy the opportunity to work in the school on a nonpaid basis. Many schools welcome this opportunity to get better acquainted with parents and to involve them in the school routine. Individualized tutoring, special work on school projects, assisting in the preparation of instructional materials are all activities that can involve parent volunteers in the school program. You should consider the possibility and particularly the benefits that will come from spending a brief period of time in the school each year. Many parents make a significant contribution to public education in their neighborhood by serving as volunteers.

Some parents have special skills and competencies that can be useful at school. Attorneys, medical doctors, engineers, plumbers, electricians, carpenters, airline pilots, accountants, and business executives can all help enrich the school curriculum by offering a special lecture or demonstration. All of these activities on the part of parent volunteers help the school in carrying out the responsibility jointly shared with parents.

YOUR CHILD'S SCHOOL AND THE SCHOOL SYSTEM

Most schools are part of a large system of schools that make up a total school district. It is important to remember that your neighborhood school is an integral part of a total school system.

The school must follow district regulations and policies set by the board of education and administered by the superintendent of schools. The principal is usually held responsible for carrying out certain regulations and policies that are uniformly administered throughout the system. Also, there is a body of school law that comes from the state legislature which must be obeyed, and officials in positions higher up in the school bureaucracy often issue directives to the school principal and the faculty. So in striving to understand your neighborhood school you must realize that it is one unit in a system that is part of the total school district and that the school district is one of many local school systems making up a statewide network of public school districts.

In most school systems each local school unit has a definitely prescribed attendance area. All of the children living within the boundaries of the attendance area must attend the school assigned unless special permission is given for another assignment. It is often necessary for school districts to change these attendance boundaries from year to year in order to keep the teaching loads in each of the school attendance areas equitably balanced. These attendance boundaries are prescribed by the local board of education. Unless exceptions are granted for good reason, your children and all the other children located in the attendance boundary will be required to attend the school assigned to them. The total number of children attending the school is usually determined by the prescribed attendance boundary.

Most school systems have a definite procedure for assigning teachers to schools. The number of teachers assigned to each school is usually determined by the number of students to be taught. Special teachers are often assigned to teach children with certain handicaps. Special personnel such as school counselors and librarians may be assigned. This is usually also done by a formula that determines the total number of personnel available to the school. If your neighborhood school has a large number of children from low-income families, your school may receive extra help and additional money from federal and state sources. Educational research indicates that children from low-income families often have greater learning difficulties. Therefore, special allowances are often made to give more individualized assistance and a richer learning program to these children.

In the Appendices at the back of this book will be found a discussion in greater detail concerning the school system and the school system bureaucracy. Should you desire to become more involved in school board elections and other matters related to governing and operating the school system, these materials will be helpful to you.

In this chapter emphasis has been given to the need to get acquainted with your child's neighborhood school. The concept of the school as a large social institution with many complex problems and numerous challenges of relating to hundreds of children and their parents has been described. A brief description of the responsibilities and pressures of the school principal and the teacher was presented to help you understand the problems of the individuals with whom you would be discussing problems related to the education of your child. A brief description of the school schedule and the need for you to understand and have a working knowledge of the school schedule was discussed.

The most important message from this chapter is the recommendation that you become intimately acquainted with your child's school and with the persons who will be working on a day-to-day basis to provide optimum educational opportunities for your child. *It is important for you to establish a free and open working relationship with the school. You must maintain continuous contact if you are to be successful in carrying out your responsibilities of lending support from your home and of providing continuous encouragement and strong motivation for your child to gain the greatest possible benefits from the program offered at school.*

5.
Understanding and Supplementing the School Curriculum

By understanding more fully the curriculum of the school, you should be able to supplement the school's efforts more effectively with your own home-based teaching activities. Many parents think of the curriculum as only the subjects taken by the student, excluding the various activities and those less formal learning programs that are not related directly to subject matter mastery. The school curriculum, however, must include all of the educational experiences that are sponsored under the authority of school officials. This includes such activities as athletics, social clubs, school plays, and special events that are planned for the general growth and development of students.

We are all familiar with the expression that experience is the best teacher. If we can think of the curriculum in terms of experience, and if we can then thoughtfully consider what experiences we need to plan for school-age children at home as well as at school, we will have begun to think in the broad perspective that is necessary in educating today's children for the future.

A BRIEF OVERVIEW OF THE SCHOOL CURRICULUM

The total school curriculum can be classified under eight broad headings. These are:

1. Language Arts
2. Mathematics
3. Social Studies
4. Science
5. Career and Vocational Education
6. Health and Physical Education
7. Arts and Humanities
8. Extracurricular activities and special programs

All of the educational objectives and outcomes can be grouped under one of these broad headings. School buildings are planned, teaching staff members are employed, and educational dollars are budgeted to support a very broad and comprehensive educational program encompassing all eight of these areas. The daily school schedule and the weekly and monthly calendars revolve around these areas. Before your child graduates from high school, he or she will have hundreds of choices to make concerning the amount of school time to spend on subjects that can be grouped under one of these eight headings. The amount of participation, the allocation of time, the selection of some subjects over others, and the degree of your child's energetic support and enthusiastic participation in these eight fields will contribute in great measure to his or her future success and happiness. The level of involvement of the home in all eight of these broad fields will determine in large measure the quality of education and the growth in human potential of each child participating in the public school program.

Parents must become more knowledgeable of the school curriculum. You must become involved with your child in the critical choices that will affect your child's future. You must lend encouragement, and you must participate in the educational dialogue that continues throughout a child's life. You must assess special talents, interests, and abilities that can be greatly enhanced by more emphasis in one of these eight broad areas.

PARENT COUNSELING AND THE CURRICULUM

You must help in guiding and counseling your child to see that talents and abilities are fully developed and that weaknesses are not neglected. No teacher or counselor at school can take on your share of the responsibility in seeing that the school curriculum fully serves the needs of your child. A teacher or counselor cannot compensate for your neglecting to participate with your child in making wise choices from the school curriculum and in seeing that these choices are fully implemented. The educational conversation at home must reflect your awareness of the broad school program and your concern that all of your children avail themselves of the opportunities that abound in the comprehensive school program covering the eight broad areas from kindergarten through twelfth grade.

John had just completed the eighth grade and was in the process of registering for courses for his first year of high school. He was a fairly able student who had carried a B average through his elementary and intermediate school years. But he had seldom displayed much interest in mathematics, and he often complained that he dreaded his arithmetic classes and disliked math.

When John came home with his tentative high school schedule, his father reviewed his course selection. He noted that John had selected a course entitled "Algebra, Individualized Study." John's father knew that he should take a special interest in his son's study of mathematics in high school because of the boy's previous lack of motivation and interest in this field. He called the high school counselor and learned that the individualized algebra course was a class designed for students who desired to study from a programmed learning text where each student progressed at his or her own speed by completing exercises designed to lead students in a step-by-step process through first year algebra. The course required a solid background in mathematics fundamentals and ability to learn without much direction from a teacher.

"Why did you select this course?" John's father inquired. "The high school counselor told me that you will need a strong interest and a good mastery of basic arithmetic to succeed in this course."

"All my friends are going to take it," John replied. "And besides that, my eighth-grade science teacher told me that his son took the course last year and really liked it. Another thing, Dad, I get bored with teachers lecturing in math classes and I get tired of watching the teacher work problems on the blackboard. This would give me a new start where I could work on my own."

"It seems to me that this matter needs more study, John," his father replied. "I will leave work early tomorrow and let's talk to the counselor and the head of the math department at the high school. Then perhaps we can make a better decision."

Following a more detailed discussion at the high school, John and his father concluded that a regular algebra class would be best for John. After they had discussed John's past problems in mathematics, the school counselor arranged for a special placement of John in a class with a teacher who had been unusually successful in making algebra interesting and in helping students who lacked aptitude and interest in mathematics. As a result of this special effort and extra concern by John's father, the following academic year was the first one in a long time when the family did not hear complaints from John about how he disliked mathematics. Although he was not the best student in the class, he enjoyed algebra and had a reasonably successful year.

The foregoing episode illustrates the need for parents to become actively concerned about the course selections that their children make in school. Parents usually know more about the individual problems, strengths, weaknesses, and attitudes that their children have toward certain subjects. When you feel that a course selection may be a mistake, you should discuss the choice in depth with your child and also get the best advice you can from the school. It is easy for children to follow the lead of friends and to select courses solely for social reasons. Without being dictatorial, parents should guide their children and serve as a source of thoughtful examination of the implications for important choices made from the offerings of the school curriculum.

LIMITLESS EDUCATIONAL OPPORTUNITY

As you consider the great breadth and depth of the American public school curriculum you should realize that your children have limitless opportunities not afforded in other countries. For example, we do not provide cutoff points to learning in a particular area. There is no critical period when a student must come before a government-administered examination for a decision concerning his or her right to continue to study in college or graduate school. In many nations a student must be at a certain grade level and pass certain qualifying examinations or the student will be prohibited from entering certain programs and pursuing certain careers and professions. In the American school system a student has an inherent right to try. He or she can continue to compete for entrance into a particular educational program. The student has a right to fail and try again. The American school system is strongly committed to the concept of educational repentance. A student can attain a record of poor performance in a specific area and still correct his or her deficiencies at a future time. This is not to say that any student regardless of ability and background will be admitted to medical school or advanced engineering study. We do have admission standards and requirements. But we do not have a time during the early teens when a child is channeled into a certain area as a result of state-administered examinations.

Our educational program is broad and flexible. It reflects our democratic ideals of providing unlimited opportunity. A student who neglects his or her studies and accumulates a questionable record can make a comeback if willing to strive diligently and put forth the effort.

EMPHASIZE SOME AREAS IN DEPTH

Students with certain tentative career objectives will want to emphasize studies in some of the eight broad field areas outlined above and take a minimum amount of course work in other areas. We live in an age of specialization where one must master a field to a point where one can perform with real authority and confidence. Such specialization must begin in the last two or three years of high school. For example, a student bound for a career in engineering or science should emphasize study in high school mathematics and science. The student should also strive to get a solid command of the English language as a tool for further study. This is not to say that a student bound for college studies in engineering or other scientific fields could not take a mimimum number of subjects in these fields and then, through diligent study and correction of deficiency on the college level, ultimately qualify for admission and attain success in the engineering or scientific field. However, a great deal of effort and painful toil could be avoided if a relatively early career decision is made.

In homes where a continuous dialogue about the school curriculum and career selection has gone on over a period of years, making a fairly early career choice will not be difficult. Students who go to school with a purpose in mind and with a specific career plan laid out will be pursuing school studies with more relevant commitment. The key to this commitment is wise counseling and guidance both in the home and at school. Constant conversation and thought and continuous exploration and investigation during the early years of schooling will lead to intelligent choices in subsequent years.

All through her early years in school Susan continuously talked about wanting to become a medical doctor. But as she entered secondary school it was obvious to her parents that medical school would be very difficult if not impossible for Susan. She did exceptionally well in English. She had a great interest in history, government, and the social sciences. Her highest marks were in these fields and in English. She barely got by in science and mathematics. In fact, she would have earned a straight A average in her first ten years of school had it not been for her poor performance in science and math classes.

Without in any way discouraging her by putting on undue pressure for more science and mathematics course work, Susan's parents talked about the heavy demands in this area of the curriculum during the last two years of high school if Susan was to follow her aim of medical school. It was explained that her four years of premedical studies would require more intense study in the very subjects that Susan disliked.

Susan's parents carefully presented some other alternatives for her consideration. They wisely avoided trying to choose her career for her, but they helped her to talk to lawyers, social scientists, social workers, and teachers. When Susan began to talk about the possibilities of a career as a lawyer, her parents helped her to see that her academic strengths would indicate many possibilities for her if she thought she would enjoy this profession. In selecting her course work for the last two years of high school, Susan realized that she would prefer to take advanced English, advanced courses in history and American problems, and to pursue studies that would lead her definitely away from the field of medicine. Susan's parents did not make this choice for her. They merely talked about alternatives, pointed out her academic strengths that led to other directions, and emphasized that her final two years of high school courses should lead her to the best possible preparation for her field of emphasis in college. With this careful, low-key guidance, Susan was able to make a wise decision that led her to a field of specialization where she had more aptitude and a higher probability for success.

Many students do not make a final career choice until after the second year of college. Indeed, others delay even longer. But for those students who can make a tentative broad field choice during the last two years of high school it is easier to make subsequent choices from the school curriculum. While a course in high school calculus would not be harmful to a student planning a career in the social sciences, it may or may not be the best choice when other alternatives are considered. A student strongly considering engineering as a lifetime career obviously would have reason to consider selecting calculus.

Parents who know the course options in school and who know the academic needs and interests of their children will be helpful counselors if they assist their children to weigh all possible alternatives and if they pay particular attention to decisions that may be unwise.

CAREER DECISIONS AND CURRICULUM PLANNING

Some educators argue that a career decision should not be made until after high school graduation. Indeed, some would argue that two years of college study should be completed before any thought is given to even a tentative career decision. The author believes that such reasoning is filled with peril for today's public school youth. A student need not make a specific and final career choice during the high school years. He or she should, however, have some general ideas about abilities and interests and should channel concentration of studies in a broad career field that can be developed into an area of specialty later on. If, for example, a student enjoys and gets along well in mathematics and science, and if the student has a great interest in a number of fields that will require a background in these subjects, this individual will be able to select a sequence of courses that may lead through advanced chemistry, physics, and calculus. The student will then be prepared to make a wide range of career choices on the college level without having to go back and take a long list of prerequisite courses for meeting admission requirements to a program of specialized study.

This study in depth on the high school level will give

meaning and purpose to the senior high school years. It will provide discipline and focus to a school career—and without narrowing and limiting options unduly. And a program that brings at least a limited amount of specialization will be much more meaningful to the student than one that covers the waterfront and provides too much general education and not enough specific concentration.

Many unusual opportunities for careers in fields not requiring a college degree are available today. Parents should explore these areas fully. Many alternatives will be found here. Too many of us think that college is the only approach to a successful life. Many career options are available through trade-technical schools, business colleges, and vocational schools of all kinds.

REMEDIAL AND CORRECTIVE INSTRUCTION

Parents should become knowledgeable about the school curriculum in order to know what remedial and corrective services might be available. Most large secondary schools offer basic skill-building courses to students with specific limitations and deficiencies. A student with learning difficulties because of reading deficiencies may dread taking a course in reading because of previous bad experiences. A knowledgeable parent will recognize this problem. The knowledgeable parent will recognize the deficiency in the student and will discuss the problem in depth at the school. Special plans can then be set forth to try to avoid a repetition of an unpleasant and frustrating school experience.

Particularly in reading and mathematics, the need for remedial assistance may be as great in the emotional and attitudinal realms as it is in the specific skill-building area. Many children are exposed to reading before they have attained sufficient readiness and maturity to learn to read. After they have learned that reading is difficult for them, the problem becomes an emotional one. Students also develop emotional blocks to mathematics; they become convinced that they cannot comprehend math and they refuse to try.

After students have matured and developed greater cognitive power, many of them benefit from remedial instruction. The problem is to persuade the older child of secondary school age to take a remedial course and to approach it with a "can do" attitude. *Many students need the services of a skilled psychologist or even an psychiatrist to help them prepare for a new attempt to master the basics in reading or mathematics. Parents should avail themselves of this assistance. Special psychological tests can be administered by these specialists to identify deep-seated fears and hostility and to pave the way to therapy that is needed before the child approaches remedial instruction.*

The main problem is that both parent and student give up too quickly. Failure that occurred several years ago should not deter you from making a new attempt to lead your child to the specialized assistance that will remedy basic learning skill deficiencies. Be sure to obtain the most capable assistance and make a fresh effort. You may be surprised at the results.

NEED FOR PARENT COUNSELING

Many parents pay little attention to the curriculum decisions of students. A child with a specific deficiency in reading or mathematics may make an unwise choice to avoid any more course work in these areas. These decisions need the support of an interested, well-informed parent.

With several hundred students to counsel, the school counselor may not be specifically aware of the child's needs. Parental indifference on the home scene and an overloaded counseling assignment on the school scene often lead to educational tragedy for the child.

The school curriculum is for the individual child. It is broad, deep, and diverse. In most school systems there are many opportunities for correction of learning deficiencies and for the building of special talents. But parents must avail themselves of all of the opportunities afforded by the curriculum. They must get involved and they must assume more responsibility for counseling, guidance, and continuous motivation and encouragement. Communication gaps between home and school must be closed. In making decisions on which courses to take and which to pass up because of time limitations, parent and child must have the awareness and initiative to take full advantage of the best learning opportunities available at home and at school. The discussions of the various offerings in the curriculum that follow should be useful to parents in helping their children gain the most from the school curriculum.

THE LANGUAGE ARTS CURRICULUM

The term "language arts" refers to the broad array of subjects offered to teach mastery of the English language in depth. It includes reading, spelling, grammar, composition, writing, speech, and literature. In a broader sense, the language arts curriculum also includes foreign languages. Most large secondary schools offer French, German, Spanish, and other languages. Indeed, many elementary and junior high schools offer some choices in these areas.

The language arts field strives to prepare a child to become literate. By attaining proficiency in reading, writing, and speaking, a child can effectively communicate with confidence. By building a rich vocabulary and learning how to express their thoughts, students attain great capacity for future learning and future development.

Parents should become interested in the child's writing progress. The ability to put thoughts down on paper concisely and with a certain degree of eloquence must be developed. Take the time to read the written compositions of your child. Ask to see specimens of the child's writing at parent-teacher conferences. Strive to learn about the child's development of language competence and do those things that will help your child to attain success and confidence in this area.

James, a seventh-grade student, was having considerable difficulty expressing himself in writing. He wrote sentences that were structurally deficient and he had difficulty organizing his thoughts and putting them down on paper. James's parents realized that he would have to gain more confidence in his ability to write. He had reached a point where he would no longer try. His experiences at school only led to further discouragement and he was emotionally unprepared to make further attempts.

When their next-door neighbors and lifelong friends moved to another city, James's parents recognized that they had an opportunity to demonstrate the need for him to write. They asked James to keep in touch by mail and to see that the family friendship was continued by correspondence. Here they could use a practical situation to motivate James to want to learn to write. It took James's mother some time to convince him that he was actually the only one who could keep his former friends posted on events at school.

As James sat down to write his first letter, he knew what news he had to tell and what items should be included. His mother helped him to make notes and to organize the order in which he would tell the events in his letter. After James had written his first crude letter, his parents read it back to him and made suggestions for improvement. They were careful to express praise as well as criticism. The letter was revised to James's satisfaction and sent off to their former neighbors.

James learned about the need for complete sentences that express clearly what one wants to say. He soon learned about paragraph structure and the need for good punctuation. His parents used this interest and practical necessity to teach a badly needed skill. When James received a letter in response, he was motivated to make further attempts at writing. This correspondence continued for a number of months, and James developed his writing ability as his parents carefully guided him. His parents had the insight to recognize a teaching opportunity. They were aware of his problems with writing because they had reviewed samples of his written themes during visits to school. They knew that the desire had to come from within their son and not from their forcing him when he had an emotional "hang-up" about writing.

This first successful attempt at writing yielded other learning dividends in the school's language arts curriculum. Other competencies were enhanced from this successful experience because James was fortunate enough to have active parents who were concerned about his problem. By being aware of the school curriculum and the deficiency in writing skill, James's parents were able to fill a learning need at home while interest was high and learning readiness was present.

Development of ability and capacity in the language arts area is fundamental to all else in education. The child must be able to read with comprehension. The child must be able to speak fluently and with full confidence that he or she can be understood and respected. The child must have a rich vocabulary and an ability to use it at home, at school, and in social gatherings. Self-confidence, social poise, ability to learn other subject matter fields, capacity to express one's thoughts in writing and in speaking are all fundamental to education. The language arts must have high priority in both the home-based and the school-based curriculum.

Parents are advised to pay particular attention to the development of language skills of each child in the home. This development begins when the child is a crib-bound baby. Parents probably play a more critical role in language development than in any other subject area of the school program. It is the first requisite for success in school and it is difficult to overemphasize its importance in the home-based and school-based learning curriculum.

THE MATHEMATICS CURRICULUM

Many educators consider mathematics to be pure logic. They believe that the child's fundamental cognitive power can be developed through mathematics. The fact that many students and adults consider mathematics to be extremely difficult indicates that more attention must be given to the mathematics curriculum at school and at home.

We live in a world of mathematics. The time that we use each day is measured. The food that we eat is purchased by dollars and is measured by weight or volume. That we live in a world of numbers, weights, measures, and mathematical computations cannot be denied. These facts must be kept in mind as the home and the school strive to build mathematic competency.

Many curriculum specialists believe that the teaching of basic mathematics is second only to language development as a tool subject that is a key to future success in all other learning. Command of the fundamental processes in mathematics is certainly essential; mathematics has been called the language of science. Even in social studies and in the arts and humanities, a fundamental background in mathematics is important. Most school programs begin with the simple and very slowly move up the ladder of mathematical difficulty. In spite of this gradual process, many students develop emotional resistance to mathematics. Both teachers and parents contribute to the attitude of resistance to mathematic studies. Most students who have difficulties in mathematics have had a few traumatic experiences that have generated attitudes detrimental to learning and harmful to proper motivation and confidence. Good teaching and sufficient individualized assistance are needed.

Parents should follow the child's progress in mathematics throughout the school years. Pay attention to the child's assignments that are brought home. Lend encouragement and discuss the importance of mathematics as a tool to be utilized throughout life. Make sure that your child's experiences are successful, reinforcing ones. Be particularly careful that attitudinal and emotional blocks to learning are not developed through learning experiences in mathematics. Seek the help of the school when necessary and offer your own tutoring services to your child if you feel capable of doing so. If not, try to arrange for tutoring if you find your child getting behind in mathematics. This is critical because of the universal need for mathematics in future education endeavors.

THE SOCIAL STUDIES CURRICULUM AT HOME AND AT SCHOOL

In education the term "social studies" refers to a broad number of very important subjects including history, government, civics, economics, political science, sociology, current events, geography, community affairs, and many other related topics. We teach the social studies to help our students gain an awareness and understanding of our American system of democracy and of our American heritage. We begin with a history of mankind and with the great and proud history of the United States. This historical perspective is essential in helping students to understand other subject matter areas in the broad field of the social studies.

The public schools aim to teach about our American system of democracy. The fundamentals of government and the individual citizen's responsibility are covered in the total social studies curriculum. The schools teach about the Constitution, the system of checks and balances, and the three branches of government. They teach about our republic and the states that make up the United States of America. They teach about other systems of government and provide a comparative appraisal of our American system. They teach about the geography of the world and how geographic circumstances make an impact upon economic and social problems of the world. They teach about politics and political parties, and about elections and election campaigns. They teach economics; in recent years there has been considerable emphasis and concern about economics and economic literacy, and this emphasis has been reflected in the field of social studies.

The schools strive to teach about the social and political problems of the current era. Course work on American problems and the great social issues facing our country are covered in the comprehensive school curriculum. The business and corporate structure of our economic system receives attention in social studies. The influence of newspapers, television, and radio is taught. The schools try to cover current events so that students will have an awareness of history in the making during their lifetime.

Students should learn how to handle controversy and how to respect competing and opposite views. They should learn about the crucial citizenship responsibilities and how they must become enlightened on issues and become involved in public affairs if our political system is to operate as it should and if our great republic is to survive. An effort is made to get students involved in current social issues. Political leaders and governmental officials are often invited to school as resource persons to help in supplementing and enriching the school curriculum. Many schools utilize newspapers and weekly news magazines as instructional materials. All of this is done to keep the instruction current and dynamically related to the unfolding drama of today's world in action.

The subjects offered in the broad field of social studies are important to all students. Both the schools and the homes that support the schools must provide an environment that will nurture enlightened citizen participation in the affairs of government. Future leaders in our country are developed in our schools. An interest in the laws of the country, in the legal profession, and in government, politics, and economics grows out of the stimulation obtained from the social studies curriculum.

THE SCIENCE CURRICULUM

Most of the public school systems of America offer a broad array of subjects in both the physical and biological sciences. This curriculum begins with simple nature study and observation on the primary school level and extends through advanced physics and chemistry at the senior high school level. Some aspect of the biological and physical sciences is usually offered every year from kindergarten through grade 12. Modern science laboratories and many new programs that offer real-life and hands-on experiences make the science curriculum in the schools meaningful to students.

The public schools strive to offer to all students the fundamentals of the life sciences and at least a broad basic background in the physical sciences. More specialized instruction and more rigorous and complex subject matter offerings are provided for those with greater interest and with career plans that require some specialized knowledge in science.

The study of science helps students to understand the scientific method and to appreciate what science has done to help provide the standard of living enjoyed in this era. Students also learn some of the fundamental scientific principles that they can use in solving problems in their environment. And the study of science should help students to develop a certain scientific attitude and to become more objective in approaching problems related to everyday life. It teaches students to rely upon evidence and to avoid jumping to conclusions that cannot be substantiated. Science teaches a certain open-mindedness and willingness to adjust to what evidence and proof teaches us. And the study of science helps students to put aside superstitions, to be curious and to be careful and accurate in making observations and drawing conclusions.

Modern science laboratories assist the schools immeasurably in accomplishing some of the foregoing outcomes. Through examining evidence and seeking proof in the laboratory, students develop the ability to think objectively and to apply scientific principles. Respect for learning and for objectivity grows out of a study of science. One learns to apply intelligence and to apply the methods of proof in solving problems. The productive and economic aspects of science and the contribution that science has made in producing the goods and services and the modern way of life we enjoy are all covered in a broad science curriculum.

Science teaching has changed dramatically over the past few years. In secondary schools the study and application of the biological sciences to modern life is covered. Many large secondary schools offer biology, botany, and zoology. Some fundamentals of bacteriology and some advanced techniques in the biological sciences are also taught in the modern high school.

Most students in the secondary school receive basic instruction in general science. Following this, those who desire to study further are presented the fundamentals of physics and chemistry. Advanced physics and chemistry are offered to those with special aptitude and career plans that necessitate more specialization. The physical science curriculum relies heavily upon laboratory work and application of mathematics skills.

CAREER AND VOCATIONAL EDUCATION AT HOME AND AT SCHOOL

Career education is a relatively new term in the field of teaching. In recent years it has become increasingly necessary for students to utilize the schools as a means to attaining economic success through employment. How does a student go about deciding what he or she wants to do as a life's work? What are the relative advantages and disadvantages of entering certain fields? What are the future employment opportunities of a specific career? What preparation is required and what subjects should be studied for certain career fields? What aptitudes and abilities of a student will suggest serious consideration of a specific career choice? The school, the home, and the community should help students to find answers to these questions. With the world of work becoming much more complex and with educational preparation for certain careers requiring early decisions on subject matter choices at school, career education becomes a necessity in the modern school curriculum. Students should deliberately study, under the sponsorship of the school, a broad range of varied career opportunities. They should become familiar with the values of our work-oriented society and should begin to seek out seriously those endeavors that will be the most satisfying and rewarding to them.

Not long ago it was not a serious matter to delay career decisions until after two or three years of college were completed. But with today's requirements for specialization, this delay in decision-making can have disastrous consequences. A few years ago many persons drifted by trial and error into a field that turned out to be a lifetime career. Such a means of decision-making is unacceptable in our modern society.

Modern school systems are offering career planning experiences for students. Students are assisted in exploring in depth a number of broad occupational fields. They are encouraged to assess their abilities realistically and to compare their interests and aptitudes with the demands of certain career fields. A much more scientific preparation for career decision-making has recently come into the school curriculum. Many high schools and junior high schools have career opportunity planning centers where students can read literature, view films, and receive specialized counseling in many fields in which young people may be contemplating careers.

Many school systems with strong commitments to career

education try to emphasize the career aspects of almost every subject offered in school. For example, a student in an English class would be given an opportunity to write some compositions on the subject matter of his career interest. In the study of biology various career fields would be explored and students would be offered an opportunity to carry out certain projects in career fields that relate to the biological and life sciences. In this context, many teachers are considered to be career education teachers as well as academic subject matter specialists in the modern high school. The exploring, studying in depth, and assessing of one's potential for various career fields require a school-wide emphasis on career education and a system-wide concern for placing students appropriately after high school, either in further study and preparation for a career or into actual employment.

Vocational education is, of course, job training and specific preparation for attaining job-entry level skills. Some educators consider the term "vocational education" to be synonymous with the term "career education." Traditionally, vocational education has not been defined as preparation for the professions. Career education, however, has been commonly considered to be education for one's lifetime career whether it be in the field of medicine or plumbing. In this sense, vocational education and career education are quite different; career education has a much broader definition and includes the total field of human work endeavor.

In recent years the American public school youth have been demanding more *relevance* in education. They want their schooling to relate to the life situations that they face here and now. They want education to be related to the real world as they know it. These demands have been changing the focus and emphasis of all aspects of the school program. There has been developing a heavier emphasis on application of what is being learned and upon the career implications of the studies. To this extent, it is safe to generalize that all of American public education has become more career and vocational education oriented.

THE PARENT AND CAREER EDUCATION

Parents should become more deeply involved in helping students to assess the potential of various careers and in helping students to prepare over a long period of time for a smooth transition from the world of studies to the world of work. The home-based educational experiences of children should include exposure to many career fields and occupations. Students should have an opportunity to talk with successful lawyers, physicians, dentists, airline pilots, chemists, engineers, architects, businessmen, electricians, carpenters, plumbers, accountants, and others who can give insight and assistance to youth striving to make a wise career decision. Parents should attempt to provide these opportunities and to help students to think objectively about this informally gathered information.

The home should start early in providing the home-based component of the career and vocational education curriculum. Total familiarity with school offerings should be sought. Encourage school officials to broaden offerings in this area and to provide deeper exploration for students before career decisions are made.

Both the home and the school should guard against premature decision-making. Students should not be pressured to make a final decision until such time as such a decision is necessary. On the secondary school level, career decisions should be tentative. Options should be kept open and students should consider certain skills acquired in high school as keys to further development. Where vocational competencies are acquired, the attitude should be one of openness and continuous progress from one job-entry ability to another.

Some schools have work-study programs in which students are offered an opportunity to receive released time from school to gain meaningful experiences in the world of business and industry. Many excellent programs of this type provide a proper mix of school-based instruction with real work experience. More opportunities of this type should be provided and student participation in them should be encouraged.

Many schools are building excellent career planning libraries. You should become familiar with the materials available in these libraries and see that your children gain the great advantages from serious study of these materials. When the student shifts from the idea of education merely for the purpose of getting to school, to the idea of education with a broad career field of study in mind, there is going to be more motivation to apply his or her education to achieving some very meaningful objectives. Career education brings purpose and meaning to all of education in the secondary schools.

Remember that both the home and the school have a

responsibility to help bring this meaningfulness and relevance of school into the lives of secondary school students as early as possible. In all of this a careful balance between premature and immature decision-making that has little meaning, and serious and mature career study, exploration, and commitment, should be maintained. The role of the parent should be one of stimulation, positive questioning, and supportive guidance. Conversation in the home should be addressed to the "education for what?" question. As the child moves along the ladder of educational progress, the guidance of the parents should be leading the student to think more and more about that time in life when one must become engaged in a lifetime career.

The total school-based and home-based curriculum should lead ultimately to a point where the student becomes an independent, self-sufficient, productive, and active adult citizen. Career education plays a very meaningful and vital role in this long and gradual process. The career and vocational education curriculum at school should be utilized by parents and students in making this gradual transformation from student to mature adult citizen.

HEALTH AND PHYSICAL EDUCATION AT HOME AND AT SCHOOL

All of the endeavors outlined so far in this chapter would be of little value to a person suffering from poor health and lack of organic vigor and physical capacity to live an active, dynamic, and self-fulfilling life. The number of physical and mental invalids in our society is appalling. The man-machine work ethic has eliminated the exposure we all need to exercise and vigorous physical activity. We should know more about our bodies and how they function. We need to recognize the value of good nutrition and sound health practices. We need to know how to preserve our health and to build our physical capacities. The broad field of health and physical education is dedicated to these crucial outcomes. Students are introduced to lifetime sports and an effort is made to teach them to recognize the value of creative recreation and an active and participating life.

The school health courses begin with the fundamentals of personal hygiene and practices of cleanliness and sanitation. The health curriculum goes on to teach about communicable diseases and how the health sciences have now brought us to the point where many epidemics either have been eliminated or are fairly well under control. The health program teaches the function of the various systems in the human body and how they perform with other systems to maintain good physical health. It also teaches about some of the social diseases and health problems related to excesses in living practices.

HOME SUPPORT OF THE HEALTH CURRICULUM

Health instruction begins and ends in the home. You should teach health by your actual practices in the home. Children should grow up understanding that there are certain things that are done for the sake of good physical health. These include eating habits and other practices around the home that will tend to preserve health.

Many schools include safety education along with health and physical education. Driver education courses have been offered to help solve the problem of massive automobile traffic, highway accidents, and resultant injuries and fatalities. Likewise, a number of safety education practices have been installed in conjunction with the health and physical education program to teach personal safety and personal security.

It is essential that the parent and school become more health conscious. There needs to be a closer liaison between the health instructional efforts at school and the health practices in the home.

THE ARTS AND HUMANITIES AT HOME AND AT SCHOOL

In a strict sense the term "humanities" includes those branches of learning covered by language, literature, and philosophy. The teaching of language and the use of the English language as a skill-building subject was discussed earlier in this chapter. However, that part of language that deals with expression of human feeling and enunciation of values in human life will be included under this heading of the arts and humanities.

In our discussion of "the arts," we intend to include the subject areas in school and at home that relate to esthetic expression of feelings. Those creative efforts in music, drawing, painting, sculpture, drama, dance, and literature will also be treated here.

The so-called useful, practical, and industrial arts were dealt with under the heading of career and vocational education.

It is extremely difficult for the school to meet its responsibility in this broad cluster of subject matter without a considerable amount of support and assistance from the home.

Those departments in school that teach art, music, and drama have a special mission. To some extent, the total school curriculum is enriched by the students and faculty participating in these fields. Schools try to teach general music and general art to all children, in order to expose them to these vital areas and to develop their appreciation for them. Then out of this program of general instruction grows the deeper exposure for students expressing interest and desire to go beyond the basic level of teaching.

Usually teachers of art, music, and drama are talented performers in their own right. This ability to demonstrate and this capacity to display a considerable amount of expressive skill are important assets to the school faculty. But a problem in this regard can emerge if the faculty member becomes too deeply engrossed in the product to the point of becoming too demanding.

Teachers of the arts and humanities must be teachers first and performing artists second. The patience, compassion, and ability to bring out the best in students must come before performing skill. A school is richly endowed if it has an arts and humanities faculty with great skill and performing capacity but also possessed of those personality attributes that make great teachers.

It is easy for a school to become so deeply involved in the public performances and displays of talents of students in special programs that real teaching is neglected. A great performing orchestra or band may not necessarily represent an outstanding program of instruction for all students in a school. In fact, it may in some rare cases represent the opposite. Distinguished art expositions that display the creative work of a few students may be impressive at the expense of neglecting many students. The arts and humanities are for all children and not just those who have innate talent or special giftedness.

PARENTAL SUPPORT IN ARTS AND HUMANITIES

Parents should aggressively support the arts and humanities in the school, both by participation and by expressions of interest and compliments. The support should also come through the home-based curriculum that plants the seeds and lends continuous encouragement toward growth in these fields. Neither the home nor the school should be considered as fulfilling its total responsibilities without a very strong program in the arts and humanities. Such programs in the home and in the school help to build a richer and deeper quality to neighborhood and community life. In our practical, economic-oriented society we must seek to build and preserve the arts and humanities.

Watch for outstanding concerts, ballet performances, and plays in your community. Also, look for opportunities to take your children to the best art galleries. Your children cannot gain an appreciation for the arts and humanities unless they have constant exposure to the finest work of our artists. In recent years the quality of TV productions in the arts and humanities has been improving. Be sure to offer opportunities for your family to enjoy some of the excellent viewing and listening opportunities currently being offered on both commercial and educational television networks. Teach your children to participate in these cultural events and to support them in your community.

EXTRACURRICULAR ACTIVITIES AT SCHOOL

For many years the public schools have sponsored clubs, student government organizations, athletics, debate teams, dramatic performances, and special music performing groups. Some schools have ski clubs, pep clubs, science clubs, home economics clubs, and certain other special interest groups. These special activities are not scheduled into the daily school program on a regular basis. That is why they are called extracurricular activities; they are outside and in addition to the regular curriculum.

The value of this activity program has been the subject of many heated discussions. Some critics call these areas the "frills" and demand that they be eliminated from the school. Others argue that they occupy so much time and attention that the regular curriculum is neglected. Some claim that emphasis is given to one program at the neglect of another. The entire spectrum of extracurricular activities is very broad and apparently well established in the public school systems of America.

Some very important extracurricular activities are carried out on the elementary school level. However, extracurricular activities occupy a smaller portion of the total time and resources of the elementary school than in the secondary school area. Additionally, senior high schools have a much broader and richer program of activities than do the junior high or middle schools. Educators have learned that teenage students have a deep and abiding interest in the activities areas. They have also learned that many of these activities provide a key to motivation. Many students would drop out of school were it not for the attraction of these school activities. From the school's point of view the activities program is vital to the total success of the school. This is particularly so on the secondary school level.

In the opinion of the author, the activities programs should be considered as part of the total school curriculum, despite the fact that credit is usually not given for participation and that extracurricular activities come outside of the regular school schedule. A total program of learning that is devoid of activities would be lacking in its power to motivate, attract, and hold students in school.

Mastery of basic subject matter, learning how to learn, and building one's total capacity to move into a lifetime career are all essential goals. No extracurricular activities program should detract from this very serious mission of the public schools. But many such activities actually provide motivation and strength to the academic program. In fact, the program of activities should be justified because of the contribution that is made to the central scope and mission of the school. If it cannot make some contribution to the total development of the child, it cannot be justified as part of the school curriculum.

PARENTAL CONCERN AND ATTENTION TO SCHOOL ACTIVITIES

You should encourage your child to participate in the activities program at school. Student government, sports, and clubs provide opportunities for socialization, for expressions of special skills and abilities, and for building citizenship. Many of the activities programs are an outgrowth of the regular curriculum. The athletic program, for example, is an outgrowth of the health and physical education curriculum. Debate, drama, and music clubs usually draw students from the arts and humanities classes. Certain career and vocational interest groups that affiliate into clubs often grow out of student study in the regular career and vocational education curriculum.

Students gain identity with the school and with the community or neighborhood that supports the school through wearing insignias and school colors that denote membership and participation in activities. It has been found that students who seldom participate in the activities program are those most likely to drop out of school. Educators have learned to use the activities program as a means of motivating students and as a device for building school spirit. Incidents develop in the activities program where subject matter taught in the regular program can be applied. For example, in student government activities, the application of the principles of democracy taught in the social studies curriculum can be made. The extracurricular activities often provide the central focus for community life. This is particularly true in small communities. As the local school strives to serve the community, many of the activity programs provide a means for carrying out civic projects and other ventures that will improve the quality of life in the neighborhood and the community. Many civic clubs and other organizations outside of the school find an opportunity to lend assistance to the school through the activities program.

You should observe carefully your children's interest and participation in the school activities program. During the elementary school years the home should stimulate an interest in activities by helping the child to be an outgoing participant. By building initial skills, talents, and interests in certain areas, the home can provide a means for future student participation in the activities program. Early teaching in the home about music, art, and drama will lead to an interest in becoming involved in clubs and activities where opportunities are provided for expression. An active family that teaches sports and participates in sports activities early in the lifetime of the child will likely produce children interested and active in the athletic program. Interest in student government and related activities will come from a home that is outgoing in its outlook and that participates in civic affairs on a broad basis.

Many desirable personality traits are cultivated through activities. Attitudes are shaped and confidence is built through success in participating with others in activities. Much of this growth begins in the home and is a reflection of the attitude of parents. You should be deeply concerned about the amount of participation and the degree of fulfillment that your children receive from activities at school and at home.

When Bill was ten years old it became obvious that he was a powerful student but that he was having problems adjusting to the social life and activities at school. While he did exceptionally well academically, he lacked the ability to participate with others and become fully involved in matters outside of the academic. Bill was deeply involved in music and displayed unusual talent. But he spent all his time practicing piano, studying in his school books, and doing almost anything that would keep him out of contact with children his own age.

After many anxious conversations about the matter, Bill's parents went to school to discuss their concerns with the principal and the teachers. School officials had also noted Bill's social deficiencies and had wondered if his parents were aware of his problem. After a long discussion at school, the parents and faculty decided to try very carefully and gradually to lead Bill into more social activity at home and at school. They planned to use his music talent for entertainment purposes in some of the school assemblies and parties. They enlisted Bill into some work with the science club. They were careful not to push too hard nor to insist if Bill declined or resisted strongly. Their approach was to make Bill feel that he was needed and to make the situation one of genuine necessity rather than an artificial or contrived demand.

Bill's parents arranged to hold a few planning meetings for student leaders at their home. They tried in other ways to increase Bill's exposure to his peers in a setting where there was little pressure but ample opportunity and mild encouragement for Bill to "come out of his shell" and interact with others.

After a long period of little or no response, Bill very slowly began to reach out to other children. As he learned to enjoy himself, he would respond more spontaneously and freely. Since he was shy and frightened, he often was the recipient of jokes and teasing. These events caused Bill to return to his old isolated position for a brief time until he was enticed by some item of special interest. He began to go outside for recess, and to stay after school for a limited number of club activities. His progress was slow, and school officials and parents had to keep gently urging him to get involved in the extracurricular activities and special events at school and in the neighborhood.

Bill gradually gained more poise and social skill at school. Although he was seldom as outgoing as most children, he did learn to participate in activities and to enjoy his participation. Through a long and patient effort and through persistence, the school and home used the activities programs to build Bill's self-confidence and social skills. This change proved to be a major turning point in Bill's life. By solving this problem prior to adolescence, Bill was, in later years, more able to cope with the problems of teenage life. The school activities program helped solve a problem that could never have been met with a program of strict academics and home-based music. Bill's parents wisely utilized the full program at the school to help in the development of their child.

SOME QUESTIONS FOR PARENTS REGARDING ACTIVITIES

It is important to emphasize that not all of the activities that are fulfilling to our children should be sponsored by the school. The home should have its own group of activities and special programs that will make a contribution toward the total growth and development of the child. Do you build family solidarity by having family activities? Do you as parents have interests that you actively pursue that are outside of the realm of your regular work? Are you involved in the affairs of your church? Do you get out to concerts, dramatic presentations, athletic events, and political rallies? Do you go on outings and picnics with your family? Do you plan systematically and regularly to build this aspect of your child's life? There is strong evidence that families that are active and outgoing in their relationships with school and community produce children who show great promise of growing into rich and productive adulthood. As parents, plan your own program of activities for your home and family life. Not only will this enrich your own enjoyment and deepen your own outlook toward living, but it will do the same for your children.

This chapter on the school curriculum and your responsibility to provide a complementary and supplementary home-based curriculum has described the broad spectrum of instruction offered by the modern public school system in today's busy world. Every subject area offered in the school and almost every activity growing out of school and family life can be grouped under one of the eight broad areas of the curriculum described in this chapter. As a parent, you should study this chapter carefully. Become familiar with each one of these eight broad areas of the curriculum. Plan thoughtfully and systematically to gain the utmost for your children from these curricular offerings. Recognize the great responsibility that you have in seeing that your home also has a broad and effective home-based curriculum that reaches into the school and gains the greatest amount of benefit for the ultimate development of your children during their growing years. Keep close to your neighborhood school. Observe the curriculum and lend support and encouragement for an adequate program of instruction. Remember that the curriculum will not be effective without your continuous positive support.

6.
What You Should Know About School Tests and Examinations

Tests and examinations are becoming an increasingly important part of school life. There is likely no other aspect of education that is more confusing to parents and frustrating to students. Test results are used to make educational decisions, to compile permanent student records, and to make decisions about promotion and placement of students. While it is important for you to have at least a few basic facts and some fundamental knowledge about tests, you should realize that tests are not the only thing to be considered in school placement and promotion. Many vital outcomes cannot be measured by tests, and educators are becoming increasingly aware of this fact. Your study of this chapter should help to put the matter of tests and examinations in proper perspective.

WHY YOU SHOULD HAVE BASIC KNOWLEDGE OF TESTS AND TESTING

As a parent you should understand a few basic facts about tests and testing in the schools. Educational testing is a highly specialized field. Without years of study one cannot become an expert. But all parents should have a fundamental knowledge about tests and how they are used in the schools.

Tests of various kinds are utilized in diagnosing learning problems, in measuring achievement, in learning about students' special aptitudes and abilities, and in determining the final grades and marks that go into students' permanent records. With the widespread use of tests and measurements in education, it is quite important for actively concerned parents to have a very broad understanding about tests and the impact that they have upon children. With this knowledge you will be better qualified to help your child. You will also be able to talk more easily to teachers, counselors, and school administrators about problems and issues in education.

Parents should be aware of the possibilities of cultural bias in tests. Because of a different background, one child may not be aware of some terms used in writing test items. Pictures of objects not common to a child's background may result in an invalid response. For example, a picture of an item of winter clothing such as a mitten may be confusing to a child raised in a warm climate. (A common test item is to show a hand, glove, or mitten and ask the student to identify it as right or left hand.) While it is extremely difficult to keep tests culturally free of bias, every effort should be made to identify items in tests that are prejudicial to a group of students.

Following is a discussion of the nature, type, and purpose of various kinds of tests used in schools.

STANDARDIZED AND TEACHER-MADE TESTS

Schools use both standardized and teacher-made tests. Standardized tests are tests that have been published by a test publishing company. They are called standardized because they have been developed to measure certain specific knowledge, traits, or abilities and they have been administered to thousands of students so that educators can easily make comparisons with students being tested. Most standardized tests come with specific directions as to how they should be administered. The tests also come with a broad and detailed data background so that educators can interpret the results and arrive at comparative conclusions. These comparative factors in standardized tests are usually called norms. From test norms your child can be compared with national, regional, and state standards.

Teacher-made tests relate mainly to the subject matter that the teacher is teaching. Most teachers have received some training in how to develop tests and how to administer them. Periodically throughout the school year, teachers will give tests that have been constructed from instruction that they have emphasized in the course work. The most common teacher-made tests are, of course, the midterm and the final examinations. Teachers utilize these tests to determine what the students have learned and to appraise their own teaching effectiveness. Additionally, teachers utilize the tests as a means of determining marks to put on report cards that are sent home to parents. Most teacher-made tests are written personally by the teacher and are printed in the school office by mimeograph or some other duplicating means.

TEACHER-MADE ESSAY EXAMINATIONS

Teachers often give essay-type examinations. In the essay examination broad questions are stated and students are requested to write several paragraphs to display their mastery of a broad subject area. Essay examinations give students opportunities to express themselves and to organize their thoughts and commit them to writing. Marking the essay examination is quite difficult. It utilizes a great amount of teacher time. Also, it is hard to be objective in scoring the essay-type examination and to assign a specific grade to it. Since the student's answer is not definitely correct or incorrect, the teacher must appraise the strengths and inadequacies of the writings of the students.

Teachers often use essay examinations to help students develop critical thinking ability. For example, an essay test may ask a student to compare two things that are alike in some respects and different in others. An examination may ask the student to express an opinion for or against a particular issue and then to discuss and defend the view expressed. Essay tests are useful in helping students to learn how to analyze and to summarize a particular matter in a few concise sentences. Following are some sample essay questions that require analysis and written expression of thoughts:

1. Describe in a few sentences how a fish and a submarine are alike and in what respects they are different.

2. Should the federal government control the sale and use of firearms in this nation? Describe the arguments for and against this proposition as you have heard it discussed in class.

3. Should public employees such as policemen, firemen, and teachers be permitted to strike? Give your views on this question and describe the opposing arguments that you have heard in class.

In scoring essay tests, teachers usually try to group the various test papers and to rate them according to their quality. By reading the examination responses and then thoughtfully grouping them according to content and comprehensiveness, the teacher can improve his or her objectivity. The teacher can also learn from the ideas that the students express in essay examinations. Such expressions give teachers clues as to what in the instructions needs more emphasis and as to what concepts in the students' thinking need to be strengthened.

MULTIPLE-CHOICE TESTS

Teachers often develop multiple-choice tests to measure knowledge that students have gained from a period of instruction. A multiple-choice question gives three to five different possible answers; the student reads the question and selects from among the group of answers the one that most accurately responds to the question.

Multiple-choice test questions require thought on the part of the student as he or she eliminates each alternative and gets down to a decision on the correct answer. The multiple-choice question may help the student having recall problems, since the power of suggestion is inherent in the list of multiple answers. This type of test is very common for both teacher-made tests and the standardized published tests. Teachers who use this format for the tests they make help students to get practice that will be useful in taking standardized tests. Following are some sample multiple-choice questions:

1. How many pints in a gallon?
   a. 4   b. 8   c. 6   d. 2   Answer:_____

2. The word *magnify* means to:
a. make it magnetic
b. make it smaller or shorter
c. make it larger or bigger
d. make it cooler or cold

Answer:_____

3. If a ribbon costs 5 cents a foot, how many feet can you buy with 35 cents?
a. six
b. four
c. ten
d. seven

Answer:_____

THE TRUE-FALSE TEST

The true-false test gives, of course, only two options in responding to each test item. A student can indulge in guesswork in this type of test, since by sheer chance the possibility of being right is 50 percent. The advantage of the true-false test is that a student can respond to a large group of items within a given period of time. These tests are easy to score but they have obvious weaknesses.

THE RECALL-TYPE TEST

Unlike the multiple-choice or the true-false test, the recall-type test leaves a blank that the student must fill in; the student must recall the answer from memory. The recall test may ask a direct question and leave a space on the paper for the student to write an answer. Another recall-type test may be written in the form of a sentence with one or more words left out. The student reads the sentence, recalls what the answer should be, and supplies the answer in the blanks provided. The advantage of the recall test is that no suggestion is made and no opportunity for guesswork is provided. The disadvantage is, of course, that the recall test item relies heavily upon memory and some memorization for responding. Following are some sample recall-type test items:

1. *A Tale of Two Cities* was written by [Charles Dickens].

2. A pound is to butter like a gallon is to [water, milk, or some other liquid].

3. There are [5,280] feet in a mile.

TEACHER FOLLOW-UP ON TEST RESULTS

Experienced teachers learn how to use teacher-made tests both for evaluation and teaching opportunities. Such teachers know that they are measuring their own effectiveness as well as the effectiveness of the learner. Test items in teacher-made tests that do not provide information about the effectiveness of the learning or of the teaching will soon be eliminated by an experienced teacher who has had years of opportunity to evaluate test papers written by students.

An obvious problem for a teacher is to construct fair, objective tests. The tests must be difficult enough to be challenging to the best students and must be easy enough to provide at least some encouragement for even the slowest learners in the class. This requires a great deal of judgment on the part of the teacher. The teacher obviously must be fair and impartial in marking the tests and in assigning a grade to each. The teacher should administer the tests in such a manner as to make the experience challenging and useful to students. However, undue pressure should be avoided and the tests should not be threatening to the extent that they generate harmful anxieties in students.

The follow-up activities on teacher-made tests are very important. Students should receive the results of their tests as early as possible after they have been administered. A student needs to know when a response was correct; this gives encouragement and reinforcement for further learning. Likewise, the student should learn about incorrect responses—not only that his or her response was incorrect, but also what the correct response is. This calls for a discussion of the teacher-made examination and for ample opportunity for students to raise questions and to profit from the testing as a learning activity.

Effective teachers are capable test makers. They not only know how to construct a good test, but they know how to utilize the test as a teaching tool. Additionally, the teacher knows how to utilize the test as a source of information that will make future teaching more effective, since the test not only tells about the students' learning but also tells about the teacher's teaching. Parents should be actively concerned about tests and test results. They should know about any problems that their children might have with tests.

Ellen was a very sensitive child. She worried about every mistake she made, and she was easily upset by pressure situations. Despite her better than average intelligence, she usually did poorly on tests. Seldom did she face a test situation calmly. She was unable to concentrate, and answers that she obviously knew were often missed.

Ellen's parents knew that her test scores were causing low marks, which were regularly entered as a part of her permanent school record. This record reflected on her ability as a student and would ultimately be harmful to her chances of gaining entrance into the college of her choice.

After discussing the matter carefully, Ellen's parents decided to make a major effort to help her do better on tests. They went to the school counselor. Following a discussion with the counselor and with Ellen's home room teacher, both parents met with the school system's pupil personnel specialists. From discussions on all these levels, it was decided that Ellen should have practice in taking sample tests so that she could become more at ease in the testing situation. She was to go through test items without pressure to build her confidence and to help her learn that tests were, after all, not so hard to take.

From a group of old tests no longer used at school, Ellen's mother gave her practice test items at home. This home-based test-taking experience was followed by a discussion of the test items, how they were worded, and how Ellen might apply her best reasoning and knowledge in arriving at answers. Ellen became familiar with the nature of tests, how they were constructed, and how best to respond.

As Ellen's parents looked further into the testing situation, they learned that she slept little the night before a test was to be taken at school. It was also learned that she often had an upset stomach and did not eat much at breakfast the morning of an examination. Ellen always studied the evening before a test. This added to her tension the following day. It was therefore decided that Ellen would do more to prepare for a test several days ahead of test day and she would not study the night before.

Ellen's parents soon learned that they had a special responsibility the day before and the morning of an examination. They became familiar with the school's testing calendar and made careful notes as to when both standardized tests and teacher-made term exams would be given. They then helped Ellen to prepare in advance, and they made a special effort to help avoid the build-up of tension the night before exams. They discussed the results of exams the day following and helped Ellen attain a more calm and objective response after testing days were over.

Ellen soon became more confident as she faced exams. She started to relax more and this helped her to give the most attention to the exam items without stress and distraction. With added confidence she gradually scored higher on exams. This was followed by compliments and reinforcement for her changed outlook and behavior toward tests. Although, because of her basic nature, she never became totally relaxed and fully confident in facing exams, Ellen improved considerably and was able to perform reasonably well in the testing situation. This resulted in her avoiding a constantly increasing record of failure, discouragement, and more apprehension.

You should pay attention to school examination time. Observe your children, discuss the testing situation, and be prepared to offer assistance. It is surprising how many seemingly intelligent parents simply ignore examinations or assume that their children need no special help or attention. There are not many events in school that merit the attention and concern posed by examinations. Most parents have a key role to play at this time but they miss the opportunity entirely because either they fail to know about the exam schedule at school or they fail to grasp the significance of these events that occur periodically in the life of every school child.

STANDARDIZED ACHIEVEMENT TESTS

We all live in a world of measurements. We get up in the morning at a certain time as measured by a clock or watch. We put on clothing that has been measured and constructed by size standards. We utilize water in the home that has been measured by a water meter. We eat food that is measured by the pound and by the quart. We travel to work in an automobile that measures the speed and gives us other measures from the instrument panel. We do our work and receive pay for our efforts by a similar measuring activity. Our total lives are touched by measurement. Measurement compares; it tells us how much and by when. We need to compare our schools with others and we need to have some means of comparing learning with others. We need standards for measurement.

Unlike a teacher-made test, a standardized test has national, regional, or statewide standards. Whereas it would be quite difficult to compare teacher-made essay examinations in English, the results of a nationally standardized achievement test measuring a student's knowledge of English grammar could be compared with the results from thousands of other students.

Test-publishing companies study the subject matter that is taught on the various grade levels in the schools. They analyze the major textbooks that are published and determine the content from these books. They interview hundreds of teachers and they go about very systematically determining what is most commonly taught in the various subjects in schools. From this information they construct test items. The wording in the test is reviewed carefully. The tests are then tried out with a small number of students. The results are analyzed and the wording of the tests are changed to make them more clear and effective. Following this procedure, a test-publishing company will administer a new test to thousands of students. From this they establish standards of comparison called *norms,* which are utilized by educators in answering the question: Compared to what?

GRADE-PLACEMENT NORMS

A standardized achievement test will have a grade-placement norm. The grade-placement norm shows a level of accomplishment that is typical for the grade level being tested. For example, the grade-placement norm for a fifth-grade arithmetic test would be 5.0. This means that at the beginning of the fifth grade the grade-placement norm that is standard for the group would be 5.0. By administering a standardized test to a group of fifth graders at the beginning of the fifth year of school, educators can compare the scores with the grade-placement norm that was established by the standardized test publisher. This gives the school some comparative information about how the students compare with the students that were tested at the time the norms were established. Obviously, approximately half of all the students who took the test would score above and half would score below the grade-placement norm at the time the test publisher was standardizing his achievement test. The students in a given fifth-grade class can get a similar comparison and the educators can see how the students measure above and below the grade-placement norm through use of the standardized test.

PERCENTILE NORMS

Another common norm or standard of comparison is a percentile score. Many parents confuse percentile scores with percentages. A percentage score on a teacher-made test would indicate that the student attained a certain percent of correct answers out of the number of test items given. *But on a standardized test a percentile score shows what percent of the students who took the standardized test scored below a given point.* For example, if in a standardized test a student scores at the 70th percentile, this means that 70 percent of the students who took the standardized test at the time it was being standardized scored below the level of this particular student. A 50 percentile score on a standardized test is that point at which half of the students scored below and half of the students scored above. A 97 percentile score would show that the student taking the test was among the top 3 percent of the students who took the test at the time that it was being standardized. In many respects a percentile score is much more important than a grade-placement score. At least, it is more easily interpreted once one has an understanding of what percentile means.

ITEM ANALYSIS OF ACHIEVEMENT TESTS

Educators pay particular attention to the items in a standardized achievement test. They want to know how well they are teaching certain skills inside of a subject area. Not only should the students be able to read at an acceptable rate, but they must also have good comprehension. They must have good word analysis ability and vocabulary skill. Educators look for patterns in all of these items so that as much information as possible will be available for purposes of analysis and correction of teaching effectiveness.

ADMINISTERING STANDARDIZED ACHIEVEMENT TESTS

Most schools administer standardized achievement tests only once each year. It is common practice not to test every grade level every year. Too much testing destroys the validity of the test. Also, standardized achievement testing is costly and time-consuming. Usually, the school system will adopt a standardized test and will determine what grade levels will be tested each year. The tests are then administered either in the fall or in the spring. The results are analyzed and given back to teachers for purposes of diagnosis and improvement of instruction.

In recent years, however, schools have been under increased pressure to show progress in student achievement. In a few situations this has resulted in standardized achievement testing at the beginning of the school year and testing again at the end of the year to measure progress. A number of private schools follow this more rigorous testing procedure and a few public school systems are now doing so.

HOW TO HELP YOUR CHILD IMPROVE IN TAKING STANDARDIZED ACHIEVEMENT TESTS

Most standardized achievement tests follow the multiple-choice format. Parents should remember this if they wish to give their children practice items for standardized test taking. The child should be coached on how to eliminate the answers that are obviously incorrect. Then the child should be taught to narrow the choice down to the best answer.

Most multiple-choice questions on standardized achievement tests offer four possible responses from which to select the correct answer. Some test publishers, however, may offer three, four, or five possible responses. Your child should learn to read the test item quickly but carefully. He or she should look for key words and phrases that actually frame the question. The test item wording is done very carefully and most items have been written and reworded several times. Every effort is made to avoid trick questions and ambiguous wording.

Most standardized achievement tests are timed. Your child should be taught to move along rapidly, so that he or she will not run out of time, and should be taught to avoid spending a disproportionate amount of time on one test item. The best way to

SCHOOL TESTS AND EXAMINATIONS

teach this to your child is to explain first that usually each test item is given the same score or weighting. Then explain that, since the tests are timed and the time is limited, it is foolish to get hung up on one test item and spend a long time on it. Suggest that the child move along at a fairly steady pace through the entire test, answering all items that he or she knows can be answered with some assurance of being correct. If the child is in doubt, he or she should leave the item until later. Then, after going through the entire test, the child should go back and work on the test items that are more difficult. If the items are multiple-choice questions, the child should try to come to an answer by eliminating the items that are the *least* likely to be correct and then put down the best answer based upon what the child knows. But this process, if it is time-consuming, should be done only after the child has responded to all items where the answer is known. It is important to discuss all of these points with your child. This background will help the child to use the allotted time wisely in a timed test.

Most standardized tests have an answer sheet that is separate from the regular test booklet. Usually, the answer sheet has simple blanks that are to be marked with either a letter or an X. Most teachers explain how to respond and make sure that all children understand how the answer sheet is to be filled out. Some answer sheets are prepared for optical scanning and scoring by computer. They require a special marking pencil and special instructions for use.

Following are some typical standardized achievement test items. By studying them you will get a better concept of the achievement tests your child will be taking in school.

Answers

1. If two boys divided a bag of *36 marbles* in *half*, how many marbles would each boy have?
_____ a. 18 b. 16 c. 21 d. 12

2. If a boy had *35 cents*, how many *5 cent* or *nickle* pieces of candy could he buy?
_____ a. 6 b. 5 c. 7 d. 8

3. How many minutes are there in ¼ of an hour?
_____ a. 30 b. 16 c. 20 d. 15

The above test items would be typical for a beginning fourth-grade level student. In reading achievement the child would read a short paragraph and then respond to multiple-choice items that would test ability to read and comprehend what was in the paragraph.

All standardized achievement tests have graduated levels of difficulty. The test items at the beginning are easy and most students are able to make correct responses. The level of difficulty increases gradually until even the brightest child reaches items beyond his or her level. Parents should explain this fact to their children so they will not become alarmed or upset.

Should you desire to give your child some practice opportunities, you *may* be able to obtain some old tests or practice items from your school. By helping your child to be skilled in taking this type of test you will be preparing him or her for many future challenges.

LIMITATIONS OF STANDARDIZED ACHIEVEMENT TESTS

Standardized tests fall far short of measuring all of the outcomes of a school, for many reasons. There is a limit to the amount of information that can be gained by testing; the number of test items are obviously limited. The standardized test may emphasize some aspects of a subject that have not been emphasized by the teacher. Some students have difficulty taking tests. Individual students may not feel up to par at the time that a standardized test is administered. Obviously, standardized achievement tests cannot measure character, social skills, and many other highly desirable human attributes that we try to develop with the total school curriculum. Parents should not, therefore, attach more significance to standardized achievement test data than would be warranted. It is very important that the limitations of the measurement capacity of these tests be kept in mind.

Some educators, however, claim that standardized achievement tests have practically no value at all. This opinion is not justified. Standardized achievement tests are probably the best measures that we have for determining how well we are teaching basic study skills in areas such as reading, English, mathematics, science, and social studies. It is important for both parents and teachers to recognize the limitations of achievement tests while using them as a source of valuable information that can help us to make our schools more effective.

COMPARING SCHOOLS BY LOOKING AT ACHIEVEMENT TEST SCORES

One of the significant findings from achievement testing has been the high relationship between the socio-economic area served by a school and the scores of students on standardized achievement tests. Schools in high-income neighborhoods show much higher scores on the tests. Schools from low-income neighborhoods and schools having a high mobility rate and a large number of minority children (children from minority groups such as black, Spanish-American, and so forth) show significantly lower scores on standardized achievement tests. The greater the number of children from these backgrounds, the lower the achievement test scores have been. It should not be inferred from this that minority children are inferior. Low-income majority children also attain low test scores. Since minorities have not generally had equal opportunity, the achievement scores have been lower.

Because of this high relationship between socio-economic factors, mobility rates, and percentages of minority children, special federal and state aid has been given to schools with high concentrations of such children. An attempt has been made to compensate children from deprived neighborhoods and from disadvantaged homes. Special programs, low teacher-pupil ratios, and individualized tutoring services have been provided. Many of these programs have been successful in reversing the low achievement factors associated with economically and culturally deprived children.

THE INFLUENCE OF THE SCHOOL AND OF THE HOME ON EDUCATIONAL ACHIEVEMENT

The school has an important impact upon the achievement of children, but it cannot reverse the influence that the home has. Children from broken homes, children from homes where English is not spoken, children who change schools several times a year, and children who grow up in an environment where learning is not encouraged enter into school competition with many serious handicaps. Educators responsible for operating schools where there are large numbers of students coming from these circumstances face an almost impossible task. By promoting closer cooperation between the school and the home, we can tend to decrease these difficulties.

As standardized achievement test scores are published on various schools, it is important to make comparisons that recognize these educational difficulties some schools face when compared to others. It is totally unfair to a school and to its faculty to compare high-income neighborhood achievement with that of a school serving large numbers of low-income and minority children. Parents must share both the blame and credit for high and low achievement of schools. In evaluating the effectiveness of the school, the contributions of the parents as well as the teachers must be taken into account. There is no greater lesson on the influence of the home on learning and on educational success than can be gained by looking at standardized achievement test data and noting the relationship that such data have to the amount of commitment that parents make to education. It should not be inferred from this that all high-income homes have strong commitment to education and that all low-income homes do not. The most humble homes can offer excellence in support of learning. The commitment is what is important.

INTELLIGENCE OR IQ TESTS

The most commonly used standardized test is, of course, the standardized achievement test. Another test almost as prominent in usage in schools is the intelligence or IQ test. Intelligence testing is highly controversial. It is also possibly the most misunderstood testing practice in American education today.

An intelligence quotient or IQ is calculated by dividing a person's mental age by his or her chronological age. IQ is represented mathematically as: MA/CA. An IQ of 100 is generally accepted as representing average intelligence. A person with a mental age of sixteen years and a chronological age of sixteen years would have an IQ of 100. Any person with an IQ lower than 100 will obviously have a mental age that is less than the chronological age.

An intelligence test attempts to measure one's *ability* to learn. Intelligence has to do with the ability that a person has to make effective use of abstract concepts in thinking and in dealing with new learning situations. It involves a high ability to generalize and a high degree of verbal thinking capacity. People with high intelligence have an ability to make successful and rapid adaptations to situations and to learn easily from experience. Persons with high intelligence are supposed to be able to learn quickly and easily.

The following table indicates IQ score ranges and indication of mental ability:

IQ	ABILITY OR CAPACITY
140 and above	Unusually bright and gifted
120–139	Superior mental ability with capability for exceptional achievement
110–119	Generally bright and capable of distinctly above average performance in school
90–109	Average mental ability ... most of human population falls in this range
80–89	Below average in mental ability ... slow learner
70–79	Usually quite retarded in learning ... needs special education service for retarded
50–69	Moron level
20–49	Imbecile level
0–19	Idiot level

Intelligence test scores relate very highly to academic achievement in school. Students who score high in intelligence generally get high academic marks in school. There are notable exceptions to this, however. There are students who are highly intelligent and who have been endowed with a great ability and capacity for learning but who have a very low commitment or desire to learn. Additionally, some students with high IQ's are emotionally disturbed and are otherwise frustrated to a point where learning is not accomplished. In such instances we have students with high IQ's and low achievement scores.

The most accurate type of intelligence test is one that is administered individually by a trained professional. Such tests are much more accurate than group, paper-and-pencil IQ tests. They utilize test items that relate closely to true intelligence with a minimum of environmental and social bias. Individually administered IQ tests by trained specialists are costly. For this reason, most schools are not able to afford to test each student on an individual IQ test such as the Stanford-Binet.

Group IQ tests taken with paper-and-pencil response to test items are used quite extensively in the public schools. Such tests do a reasonably effective job of making a rough approximation of intelligence. Individual students, however, may vary greatly in how they score in a group IQ test. Most of the better group IQ tests that are administered in the schools correlate very highly with individualized IQ tests such as the Stanford-Binet. But educators are still quite cautious about the use of group IQ tests, since any individual student may, because of a unique circumstance on the day of the test, get a very poor score that is not at all representative of his or her intelligence. Group IQ tests are more useful in assessing the capacity of an entire class and in screening students who may score at some extreme point, as a means of identifying individuals who may have special learning problems. Through use of the group IQ test as a screening device a few individuals can be identified and receive an individually administered test. Generally speaking, group IQ tests are used for screening purposes and for getting general information about a broad group of students. The individual IQ test administered by a highly trained specialist is then utilized for diagnostic purposes.

IQ test items attempt to measure mental ability as contrasted to knowledge or learning achievement. Following are typical items found in IQ tests for elementary school age children:

1. The examiner says to the student: "Listen to these numbers carefully and repeat them backwards. For example, if I said 8, 9, 10, you would say 10, 9, 8. Now listen carefully to these numbers and say them backwards:"
    8,   3,   7,   4
At a certain age, the examiner may give the child a second try but will use another set of four numbers such as:
    6,   2,   5,   9
The number of digits to be repeated would be increased as the test progressed to a higher level of difficulty.

2. The student is asked to explain such things as how a clock and a calendar are alike and how they are different. Other similar tests of cognitive capacity would be presented.

3. The student is asked by the examiner to respond to analogies such as:
    a. shoes are to feet as gloves are to [hands].
    b. water is to a pump as blood is to the [heart].
These analogies may be very simple for younger children and

increase in complexity with increases in age. Test items such as these are quite common in IQ tests.

  4. Those who prepare IQ tests try to limit them to items that require the use of logic and mental capacity, and they try to keep to a minimum questions requiring *specific knowledge*. They avoid factual questions per se, but it is obvious that tests cannot be constructed that are entirely devoid of fact. For example, the following items would be found in IQ tests that require some prior knowledge (even though the emphasis is on the mental power required to produce the correct answer):
  a. If you had a basket filled with 36 eggs and you stumbled and broke 2/3 of them, how many eggs would you have left?
  b. If you took 80¢ to school for lunch and you gave your friend 20¢, what fraction of your lunch money would you have left?
  c. A boy took his girl to the movies. He had $10.00. The tickets cost $1.50 each, and they each had a hamburger that cost 50¢ each. How much money did he have left?

These types of questions, the analogies given above, and the tasks such as repeating sequences of numbers backwards are typical of items found in most IQ tests. Through years and years of experimentation and through comparison with results from thousands of students, the IQ test builder has been able to construct a somewhat crude yardstick for measuring intelligence. There is a high correlation between capacity to learn and high scoring ability on test items such as these.
  Some of the more complex, accurate, and sophisticated IQ tests include drawings or actual objects that can be displayed and demonstrated by the examiner for response by the person being tested.
  It requires special training and a considerable amount of practice to administer and score IQ tests.
  Most children with average intelligence can be successful in the public schools. Motivation and a good self-image are much more important traits and these are what should be occupying the concern of parents. Most people utilize only a small part of their total intellectual capacity. Therefore, any individual with normal intelligence can apply himself with reasonable diligence and be successful. In modern education we are learning more and more

that motivation, drive, and high commitment can compensate manyfold for a small deficiency in endowed mental capacity.

EARLY CHILDHOOD EXPERIENCES INFLUENCE IQ

Not many years ago educators believed that intelligence was inherited or fixed at birth. Recent research from cognitive psychologists, however, has encouraged us to believe that *we can help a child actually to increase his or her intelligence if the child is exposed to certain mind-nurturing experiences early in life.* During the first five years of life a child should be stimulated to use his or her mental capacity and to learn how to learn. Since most of a child's basic intelligence has been formed by the time school age has been attained, parents of preschool children should pay particular attention to early learning experiences of their children. A complete program of home-based preschool education has been developed by a number of educators, and parent guides and manuals have been published. Parents of preschool children should become familiar with the programs available and should offer the recommended experiences to their preschoolers.

It is important for parents of school age children to remember that each child is endowed with a different learning capacity. Avoid making comparisons between your children insofar as academic achievement and learning capacity are concerned. Each child should be accepted with his or her own abilities and talents. Pressure should be avoided, and each child in a family should be encouraged and supported in his or her own learning style within the framework of individual abilities. Many children who seem to be slow in the academic situation blossom and attain unusual heights of accomplishment in later life. Furthermore, children with the same father and mother can still have a widely varied heredity. Interest and aptitudes vary considerably and the wise parent guides each child as a separate human being with unique strengths that can be utilized through wise and insightful teaching.

ADVICE TO PARENTS ON TESTS AND TESTING

Many decisions affecting your child will be made on the basis of the child's scholastic record attained through the years of schooling. Much of this record is influenced by how well your child does on teacher-made and standardized tests. Scholarships, distinctions and awards, and acceptances in some college-level programs (such as law school, medical school, and other graduate school programs) are all given partly on the basis of examination scores. Successful students simply must learn how to take examinations and do well in the testing situation. Remember and put into practice the following ten ideas as you help your child meet the challenge of both standardized and teacher-made tests:

1. You can be of great assistance to your child by becoming informed about examinations, admission tests, and requirements that must be met by examination.

2. Become conscious of the critical dates when your child will be taking key exams and lend your wise assistance at home. Encourage, but do not pressure.

3. Offer practice opportunities in advance if you know that your child needs more familiarization and more contact with sample test items.

4. Learn about opportunities for orientation courses, seminars, and other events that might be offered.

5. Plan your home activities so that they will not compete with or be harmful to your child's school exam schedule.

6. Be careful not to pose as an expert after you have attained a little knowledge about educational tests and measurements. But know enough so that you may be helpful.

7. Be sure to use your right to see your child's permanent record at school and pay particular attention to standardized tests. *Remember that under the freedom of information laws passed by Congress and some state legislatures you have the right to examine all of the official school records and test scores that are part of that record.*

8. Do some studying on your own about tests and testing. This will help you to help your child.

9. Try to be a source of inspiration, common sense, and

constant encouragement as your child competes in the world of educational tests and measurements.

      10. Know about all the opportunities and avail yourself of them.

We have not discussed the many other forms of specialized testing such as aptitude, attitude, personality, and psychological tests. These relate to a highly specialized field of educational diagnosis beyond the level of discussion in this book.
      Educational tests are vital events in the lives of schoolchildren. Parents are particularly uninformed about this part of the schoolchild's life. Education is advancing along with other fields, and as we gain a greater scientific basis for educational practice we are going to see an increasing frequency in the use of tests. Even in the current state of education practice, tests are used extensively for many decision-making purposes. Since these decisions will influence your child's future, you should be actively concerned with the task of helping your child.

7.
Counseling and Guiding Students at Home and at School

You have a responsibility to offer wise counsel and continuous guidance to each child in your family throughout the critical school years. In the field of counseling and guidance too many parents depend on the school to assist the child in making wise educational decisions and in making social and psychological adjustments. Most schools have extremely limited counseling staffs. It is most unwise to expect these heavily loaded counselors to carry the burden of offering individualized counsel to every student. With the resources available to most schools it can't be done.

Counselors in our public elementary schools are almost nonexistent at the present time. Very few elementary schools have even one full-time counselor. What elementary school counseling is done must be accomplished by the principal or by the student's home room teacher. Most of the counseling on the elementary school level is group counseling where an entire class is oriented to the school's educational program. This is not to say that many fine teachers will not be found giving individualized help and personalized assistance to children. Many dedicated teachers do an excellent job of rendering advice and counseling assistance to students on the elementary school level.

Secondary school counselors are found in most junior and senior high schools. However, a typical counselor-student ratio is about 400 students to one counselor. A few of the wealthier school systems in the United States may have a counselor-to-student ratio that is as low as 200 to one. With a counseling load of this magnitude, a counselor is under constant pressure. Unfortunately, most of the counselor's time is taken up with problems related to students who are having serious difficulties in school. At registration time, when students are selecting classes, and at other times during the year these heavily burdened counselors do find time to render some assistance to the normal or average child. But continuous, personalized, in-depth counseling by these trained professionals is difficult to provide because of the heavy student load that each carries.

There simply has not been sufficient money in school budgets to employ enough trained counselors. The basic instructional staff is, of course, an absolute necessity in school. When the budget pressures on these priorities and on supplies and textbooks are met, there is very little money left to employ counselors. For this reason, parents committed to providing the highest quality educational opportunity for children must take an active part in the counseling and guiding aspect of education. In this chapter we will discuss the school counseling and guidance program and also make suggestions and offer some explicit advice to parents concerning home-based counseling and guidance.

SUGGESTIONS FOR HOME-BASED COUNSELING AND GUIDANCE PROGRAM

It is the parents' responsibility to guide children through the period of growth covering the time from a tiny baby's total dependence upon the parents to a point where almost complete independence has been attained. Self-reliance should gradually grow each month of a child's life. Keep this goal in mind as you carry out your responsibilities in the field of counseling and guidance. Following are fundamental concepts that should guide your counseling activity with your child:

1. *Everything you do for your children and everything that you help them do for themselves should reflect your ultimate goal of leading them to independence and self-reliance.*

2. Gradually shift more and more responsibility over to your child as he or she grows older.

3. Change your thinking and gradually change your relationship to your children as they grow older and become capable of more responsibility.

4. Maturity comes through confidence that one builds in oneself.

5. Confidence in oneself comes from actual experiences in handling many responsible tasks and in meeting interesting challenges.

6. To guide your child gradually to maturity, systematically shift added responsibilities over to your child's shoulders. Do this with an expression of considerable confidence and with loving care and compassion.

The following episode illustrates the problem created by parents who do too much for their children:

John, aged 17, was a young man who had just completed the eleventh grade. John and his mother were very close. Because of a severe illness when John was five years old, his mother had constantly considered him to be frail and in need of much protection and assistance.

John failed to complete his driver training course in high school. He was able to pass the written work, but he lacked the self-confidence to drive competently on the road. When John's father had a conference with the high school principal, the counselor, and the driver training teacher, his eyes were opened to some problems that needed his attention. He learned that John called his mother several times each day. If he failed to call, his mother was almost certain to call or drive over to school.

"John hasn't had an opportunity to learn how to make his own decisions," the counselor suggested. "He calls his mother on every little decision or problem. And his mother is constantly calling him."

"We think John has enormous potential," the principal added. "He is bright. His capacity to learn is limited only by his fear of failure. We think he leans on his mother too much. He needs to strike out on his own and do some things from start to finish with no help from his mother."

"I agree," the driver training teacher added. "He tried to do all his behind-the-wheel practice after school. He asked several times to have his mother come along and ride in the back seat. I refused to allow this because I felt he should master this skill independent of his mother."

"John and his mother are very close," John's father said. "His mother almost lost him when he was five years old. They cling to each other. There is no doubt about that. But I never dreamed that he was so totally dependent on his mother. His school marks have always been very high."

"How much time have you spent with John?" the principal asked. "Do you ever give him a job to do on his own? Have you ever gotten him involved in a project where you help and he leads out and makes the decisions?"

"I've been too busy," John's father replied. "I've left all of this up to my wife."

We gain confidence by doing things. One success gives birth to another. Young people need—above almost everything else—self-confidence. We destroy this when we overpamper, come to the rescue too quickly, and constantly smooth the road. John's mother meant well. She wanted to guide her frail child and protect him from life's cruelties. But this weakens over the long haul because it destroys self-reliance.

Maturity and independence require intellectual competence and emotional stability. A mature person in the late teenage years gets to this point through having shouldered more and more responsibility. Certainly teenagers in the tenth, eleventh, and twelfth grades in school should have attained the maturity to earn and manage money. A teenager of this level should be able to manage his or her own time and to meet appointments without parent assistance. Teenagers should be able to plan ahead to meet emergencies and to cope with unforeseen difficulties by managing time and money wisely. Many important decisions should be made by teenage youth without extensive adult help.

HOME COUNSELING OF TEENAGERS

Too many parents do too much for teenagers. Earning and managing money must be learned through experience, and can best be learned in the home. Ability to keep appointments, to be punctual, and to work out one's own daily calendar must be learned. Parents who plead with teenagers to get up in the mornings and to get to school on time usually weaken rather than strengthen the abilities of these youth to meet responsibility. A teenage youth should be provided with an alarm clock and should be given the responsibility to get up and prepare for the day's activities without excessive parent coddling. Parents who constantly "bail out" teenage students from financial difficulties are guiding these youth in the wrong direction. Counsel and guide your youngsters to more mature action by placing the responsibility where it belongs. Many parents who think they are being kind to their children are actually mistreating them by creating an artificial environment around the home that will truly make it difficult in later years when total independence is demanded.

Most parents are well-meaning. Many things they do are habitual, from an earlier time in the lives of their children. Parents must "shift gears" as the child moves up to the age of youth and young adult responsibility. This shifting should be gradual into junior high school and should be more pronounced by the time the youth enters senior high school. During the high school years one may be a counselor when one is needed, offering words of advice from time to time. But parents should stop controlling all of the youth's decisions and behavior. This is a time for wise counseling coupled with a gradual loosening of controls.

CONVERSATIONS WITH OLDER CHILDREN AND YOUTH*

The conversation between parent and teenager must reflect this determination to help the student grow to maturity. Teenagers must be treated with more respect and confidence when they reach this age. They are certainly capable of carrying on adult conversations when they arrive at this level of maturity. This is a good time to talk about family finances and to discuss some of the

---

*For an excellent treatise on conversing and relating to teenagers, see Haim C. Ginott's book, *Between Parent and Teenager* (New York: The Macmillan Company, 1969).

worries and apprehensions of managing a home, paying the bills, and meeting the obligations of the family. To help your teenager grow to maturity, bring your young man or woman along with you in your conversation. Let your teenagers know about your work, your business affairs, your successes, and your failures. Talk about matters that are on the minds of many adults. Delegate adult responsibilities. As you do this, you will truly be offering the kind of incidental counseling and guidance necessary to lead the teenage youth in your home toward a natural transition to full maturity.

Parents of teenagers should plan for a series of mature conversations that are open, candid, warm, and supportive. These young people should be led to talk about the new emotions, sex drives, yearnings, and worries that come with teenage living. Surely this is a turbulent time in the life of any person. As a parent counselor you should plan to help your youth move through the teenage years as smoothly as possible. As a parent, you should strive to build the rapport that will admit you to the youth's inner feelings and concerns. This is the gateway to true parent counseling. You must establish this relationship if you are going to be effective. You must reach this point of true confidence and understanding if you are going to carry out your counseling and guidance responsibilities during this period.

It is difficult for parents to shed the role they played in the earlier years when they disciplined, controlled behavior, protected from injury, rewarded for good and punished for bad performance. But much of this role must be changed when the teenager reaches fifteen or sixteen years of age. You must admonish less. You must not nag and lecture. You must chat casually and sincerely. If you are to get close to your teenager's feelings and inner thoughts, you must admit this young person to some of your thoughts and feelings.

Following are six important points to remember:

1. Beware of an impulse to lecture to teenagers.

2. Don't recriminate.

3. Don't get uptight when your young man or woman reaches out and breaks the barrier from childhood to almost adulthood.

4. Trust your youngster and let him or her know that you do by actions as well as words.

5. Don't be too nosey and don't be too eager to know too much from your young man or woman.

6. Give your teenager some privacy.

If you haven't reached a point where your teenage youth can largely be trusted, you won't help the situation by prying into private matters and demanding to control all of the behavior and all of the decision-making. In fact, you hang on to your teenage youth by turning him loose a bit and by expressing confidence in his or her decision-making capacity. It is true that the way to keep closer to your child and to have an opportunity to counsel and guide him or her in the teenage years is to permit some differences of opinion and some drifting away from time to time.

WHAT TO AVOID IN COUNSELING TEENAGERS

Parents functioning in the role of parent counselor should keep out of teenage fights and struggles except when asked for help or when disaster is imminent. Try to offer counsel when an opportunity presents itself, but do not insert yourself into some of the inner difficulties that go on in the teenage world. Put in a subtle word here and there, but keep your distance from many of the struggles that are a normal part of teenage life. A wise parent counselor observes from a distance on some matters. Wise parents know that some lessons come only from the old-fashioned school of hard knocks. This does not mean that we do not stand ready to help and to provide guidance. But it does mean that we cease to hover over our children when they are teenagers and we step back a distance to permit some experiences to mellow and mature the young man or woman. This is admittedly hard to do when a parent loves a child and aches to help a youngster who is facing troubles. But it is absolutely necessary that parents restrain themselves from an impulse to carry out the role that has been theirs up to this point.

PARENTAL COUNSEL ON SEX MATTERS

Make sure that your teenage youth enter into the turbulence of puberty and develop the physical capacity to become parents with a sufficient factual background about sex and human reproduction. Too much is shifted to the church and school in this area of responsibility. *The best place for sex education is in the home, and well-informed parents can be the best teachers.* This statement cannot be valid if parents are not informed. But parents wise enough and interested enough to earn a living, establish a home, and rear children can learn about sex and human reproduction and teach it to their children. This is a parental responsibility and you should not try to shift it to someone else. Parents should, of course, seek assistance from church leaders, physicians, school officials, and others. But as you examine your role as parent counselor to your teenage children, you must not neglect your prime responsibility for the delicate teaching about the human body's sex urges and the reproductive system.

Don't neglect this responsibility, and don't delay too long. Your failure may result in some tragic mistakes for your teenagers. Teenagers will get information about sex from somewhere. Make sure that it comes from you and from your home and not from some crude and poorly informed source. Think seriously about this responsibility as you ponder your role as parent counselor to your teenage youth.

WATCHING FOR CRISIS SITUATIONS

As a parent counselor pay close attention to your child's mental health. Watch for signs that your child may be refusing to face and live in the real world. Look for these kinds of emotional crises and strive to be a close and willing counselor. Help your child to be positive, to think well of himself or herself, and to be confident of his or her abilities. Do not add to the pressures by expressing your own apprehensions. Be wise enough to seek professional assistance if you find that your child is having extreme emotional difficulties and manifesting some serious mental health problems that apparently cannot be alleviated by normal means. It is always wise to seek the asssistance of a professional when you feel that you have done about all that you can. If you can't afford professional assistance, ask the school for help. School officials usually have many contacts with other agencies that can give some financial help. They are usually willing to do this if you are sincere in your concern and desire to help your youngsters.

You should strive to know the symptoms of extreme

emotional disturbance and poor mental health. Of course, some stress and difficulty are part of normal living. But you need to know the difference between being temporarily disturbed and being under enormous stress to a point where considerable psychological damage can be caused. Be a guardian of your child's mental as well as physical health. Take the time to learn and to observe so that you can carry out this very important aspect of your responsibility as parent counselor.

NURTURING IDEALS

Try to help your child to grow spiritually while growing intellectually and physically. Lead your children to the church of your choice and keep them close to high levels of spiritual idealism. This can be done by example, by a highly moral life and a high standard of conduct in your home. It can be done by recognizing the nature of man as compared to other forms of life. Point out such aspects of life as you observe it. Express your own confidence in your child's basic good nature and capacity for lofty ideals and buoyant spiritual living. It is, of course, useful to build the spiritual side through fine art, literature, and music in the home. Insist upon clean speech, high moral thinking, and the highest standards of conduct around the home and you will lead your children to true spiritual growth.

LOOK AT PROMISING CAREERS REQUIRING SKILL TRAINING AND TECHNICAL EDUCATION

Many parents fail to assist young people to consider some very promising and rewarding careers requiring less schooling than a college degree. There are many outstanding careers that require special ability and preparation. A diesel mechanic, for example, is usually paid a higher salary than many who have a college degree. Laboratory technicians, electronics specialists, and other fields may offer the young man or woman in your family a very promising and personally satisfying career.

In your home-based career counseling efforts don't give the erroneous impression that all good and prestigious jobs are in the professions and require college degrees. Learn all you can about technical institutes, vocational schools, and community and junior college programs that offer excellent training in fields that are in high demand, pay good salaries, and offer very satisfying job opportunities.

Particularly in our American society, we have mistakenly ignored many promising career fields. Wise parents encourage consideration of all career opportunities, and they carefully avoid the errors of many who think that the best jobs are found in college degree fields.

HOW COUNSELORS WORK IN THE SCHOOL PROGRAM

In most school systems the counseling and guidance program is under the direction of a director of pupil personnel services. This director usually serves as a key member on the staff of the superintendent of schools and is most likely to be found in the school district administration building. The director of pupil personnel services gives leadership and direction to the counseling program throughout the school system. He or she visits the various schools and discusses the counseling and guidance program with the principal and with the counselors assigned to work under the direction of the principal. The director of pupil personnel services holds in-service training meetings with the counseling staff in the school system and provides continuous direction for the program of counseling in the school system.

In most large school systems the director of pupil personnel services will have a small staff of specialists. School psychologists, social workers, and tests and measurements specialists are usually assigned to the pupil personnel services department of a school system. These staff members work on special problems that are beyond the capacity of the ordinary counselor to handle on the local school level. Most school districts have a referral system whereby principals, counselors, and teachers can refer students with unusual learning difficulties or extremely difficult behavior problems to the central pupil personnel services staff for special diagnosis and assistance.

The counseling and guidance staff in the school works under the direction of the principal. However, both the principal and the counseling staff receive some assistance and leadership from the director of pupil personnel services.

The counselors in the school are usually assigned a specific number of students as a counseling load. Ordinarily the counselor-student ratio is about 400 students to one counselor. As was indicated earlier, this load is far too heavy but it is about typical for most schools laboring under restricted budgets.

Counselors have a prime responsibility to help students to make decisions on what classes they should take as they register for school work. In the offices of most counselors will be found the students' permanent records, which are discussed in the next section. These record folders contain information of value to the counselor as he or she helps the student to make critical decisions about priorities on classes to take and where to place emphasis in building an educational program leading to a long-term career objective.

Many students are able to make school enrollment decisions and to sign up for classes with very little assistance from the counselor. Teachers are, of course, available for assistance to students. Many students have a better opportunity to get acquainted with a teacher from whom they have had a considerable amount of instruction than with a counselor. For this reason, many teachers are closer to some students than is the counselor. However, even in these situations, both the teacher and the student might find occasion to receive specialized help from the counselor. In this sense, the counselor is often called on to assist the teacher as well as the student in helping to arrive at wise educational decisions.

THE PERMANENT RECORD FOLDER

The student's permanent record folder, which is usually kept in the counselor's office, contains a transcript of the student's academic record. The courses taken, the grades earned in each course, a record of absences and tardies, and other pertinent information related to academic achievement and attendance will be found in this permanent record folder.

In most school systems an IQ score, standardized achievement test data, and interest and aptitude test information will be found in the permanent record folder. Information concerning activities, special accomplishments, special projects, and hobbies may also be stored in this folder.

In circumstances where students have special problems, information concerning psychological tests, special diagnostic analysis, and more in-depth records that will shed light upon the problems and accomplishments of students will also be found in the permanent record folder.

GAINING ACCESS TO SCHOOL RECORDS

Educators in general and counselors in particular have had some unusual experiences in discussing the contents of the student permanent record folder with parents. Many times parents arrive at erroneous conclusions after having reviewed the contents of a student folder. Without specialized training, the lay person can easily misinterpret sensitive information such as IQ and achievement test scores. Because of this past history in the field of education many counselors have been reluctant to display the contents of the permanent record folder to parents. It is the author's belief that many school officials have been far too secretive about permanent record folders. The key to better and more effective education is to establish a closer working relationship between the parent and the school. Both parents and students need to know more about the student's educational record. While school officials should be careful to avoid divulging private and privileged information to anyone, older students and parents need to have as much information as they can get. More openness and free access to student personnel records must be accompanied by a higher level of parent and student use of such information. By means of some diligent study and willingness to become better informed, many parents can make a great contribution to the educational process by learning more about the educational records and achievement of all children in the family. Recent federal and state laws guarantee parents and mature student access to their records. Parents should be aware of these rights.

ADVANCED PLACEMENT PROGRAMS

Some students strive to earn college-level credit by taking advanced placement classes and by competing in specially developed testing programs while in senior high school. Many students are able to enter college with college-level credits already on the books. Records of advanced placement courses and special, collegiate-level testing activity are also kept in the permanent record folder of the student. Many counselors use the permanent record folders to identify students that should be encouraged to take advanced courses and accelerate themselves along the educational path.

IMPORTANCE OF A GOOD SCHOOL RECORD

When a student leaves high school and enrolls in a vocational institute, junior college, senior college, or university, much of the information in his or her permanent record folder is transmitted to the post high school institution. There is almost always a transcript of credits that indicates the courses taken and the marks that were earned for each course. Other specialized test scores and information concerning special interests and activities of the student may also be transmitted if it is requested.

Parents should constantly encourage their children to build a good record in the public schools. This educational record may be the key to future opportunities.

GROUP COUNSELING

Because of the heavy counseling loads of most counselors, students are often offered group counseling services. In group counseling sessions students receive information concerning career opportunities and post high school planning. They are also often instructed in such matters as how to relate effectively to others, how to share responsibility and get a group to work toward common goals, and how to solve problems and conflicts that arise among groups of students. In some instances it is educationally sound to work with a small group of students having a common problem. Counselors often organize small discussion groups where difficulties can be aired and students can share with each other in understanding problems and arriving at solutions.

There are obvious limitations to group counseling activity. Many students need highly personalized attention. Many problems that students have were created in group situations. For this reason, sometimes group activity may be counterproductive. Counselors and school psychologists generally recognize the limitations of group counseling and strive to utilize the techniques wisely.

HOME ROOM COUNSELING ACTIVITIES

In most schools groups of students are assigned to teachers who are responsible for offering special guidance and counseling. These groups are usually organized in a home room type program. Periodically throughout the school year students report to a home room teacher—approximately thirty to a classroom—where they receive instruction and also avail themselves of opportunities to raise questions. Most home room programs take care of the routine matter of explaining graduation requirements and typical school rules and regulations. Home room teachers are encouraged to get to know their group of students as well as possible. This teacher then becomes the advocate and special teacher assistant to the students under his or her judisdiction.

With heavy teaching loads, there are obvious limitations to the effectiveness of the home room teacher program. Many teachers are so heavily burdened with day-to-day teaching loads that they do not find the time to respond to all of the needs of the students assigned to them. But in many schools the home room teacher program is highly effective in giving the student a sense of belonging as well as the realization he or she can come to at least one person in the school who will function as a special advocate.

Home room teachers often receive instruction and assistance from counselors. Because of the heavy counselor-student ratio, many schools utilize the home room teaching program for some counseling activities. The counselor then serves as a specialized assistant to the teacher and as a resource person with responsibility to transmit information and direct the success of the home home room teacher program.

INDIVIDUALIZED COUNSELING AT SCHOOL

School counselors spend many hours in individualized counseling service. Students are referred to the counselors by teachers and other staff members for specialized assistance. Often students themselves come into the counselor's office for individualized help. The face-to-face counseling situation is, of course, the most effective.

Unfortunately, it is usually the student in trouble who receives the individualized help. Most of these students are from homes where parents have neglected their responsibilities;

therefore the obvious injustice of the troubled or trouble-making student's receiving the individualized counseling is compensated for by the fact that these students need the help the most and receive it the least from home.

A counselor must establish a special relationship with students receiving highly personalized counseling assistance. If a counselor receives a reputation for talking about highly personal matters that were discussed in private, he or she will usually be shut off from candid and open discussion with students. When this happens the counselor's effectiveness is badly damaged. For this reason, counselors are usually very careful about discussing information that has been disclosed in confidence. Important assets to the counselor are *confidence* and *credibility*.

Counselors are usually well informed about special services available in the school district and in the neighborhood and community. Most counselors wisely ask for assistance from other highly skilled professionals. Counselors often have occasion to call parents in for a confidential conversation on matters related to their children. Most counselors view the parents as an additional resource to be utilized in helping children to gain the best in educational opportunity and in educational decision-making.

The role of the school counselor is a very critical one. Most counselors have spent years in specialized training. They carry a heavy burden and provide vital links between the student, the teachers, and the homes. We need many more counselors in our schools, but with limited budgets we must get parents involved more deeply in carrying some of the counseling and guidance responsibility for students.

Parents should pay particular attention to the content and the quality of counseling offered at school. While most counselors are well trained and use sound judgment in counseling, the parent should guard against the exceptional situation in which the counselor is not wise nor realistic in suggestions and advice offered. Be in touch with your youngster; get feedback on how his or her interviews are going, and offer assistance. Constant communication with both the school and the youth is essential.

CAREER INFORMATION AND THE COUNSELING PROGRAM

Career education was discussed in Chapter 6. However, counselors have a special role in the career education program.

Almost every aspect of the educational program will be more relevant to the lives of students if the program has some career education in it. Students must gradually and steadily arrive at a level of mature thinking where serious career decisions can be made. Counselors must become leaders in the career education movement. They must become even more knowledgeable about all aspects of career planning. Counselors should give leadership to teachers and should offer specific suggestions that will help the various instructional departments in the secondary school to offer career orientation in classes in English, science, mathematics, social studies, the humanities, the arts, and other subject matter areas of the curriculum. The counseling staff should assist the total school faculty to assume more responsibility for career education. Each faculty member should be helped to assume a role as a career educator as well as a subject matter teaching specialist. Each modern secondary school should develop a career education program, and a major responsibility for executing and coordinating this program must emanate from the counseling and guidance offices of the school.

8.
What to Do When Your Child Is Failing in School

All parents hope that their children will do well at school. When our children have difficulty or when they do not measure up to our expectations, we wonder if there is something wrong with the child and we also wonder if the school is doing its part. We sometimes blame the child's teacher. We sometimes blame ourselves. We often wonder if we are doing what we should as parents in helping the child to succeed at school. *It is very important that we examine ourselves as parents and that we study our relationship to the child.*

     As you read the recommendations in this chapter, the task of helping your child if he or she is failing in school may seem to be a most formidable one. But remember that the ideal described is seldom reached by parents. You should not be discouraged nor feel that you have failed if you know that you cannot do everything suggested here. You may find that you are already carrying out a number of the common sense ideas and that you will (with a little extra effort) be able to follow many more suggestions.

Learning is a very complex process. Emotions and attitudes cause most of the learning problems that children have. When a child is having difficulty at school, he or she is often suffering from emotional problems. The child's attitude and motivation may be at the root of the difficulty. Most behavior and learning problems have a cause. In many cases the cause may be very complex, made up of a whole series of problems. Should your child not be realizing his or her full potential, it is your responsibility as the child's parent to take some immediate action to remedy the difficulties.

GETTING ALL THE FACTS

Like most busy parents, you may not have the time to take an extensive inventory of facts concerning your failing child. The paragraphs that follow raise questions and offer suggestions that should enable you to think readily of some unmet needs that you can help to provide to your child. If your child is failing at school you obviously will want to learn as much as possible about the teaching and learning situation at school and at home. You will want to think carefully about your child's feelings, attitudes, physical condition, and mental health. You may want to learn more about your child's records and files at school. And you will most surely want to examine yourself and your own personal relationship to your child. By stimulating your thinking about your child through leading your thoughts through an extensive list of questions you may discover a number of action steps that you can take immediately to help get your child back on the road to success in school. As you read through the questions that follow, do not feel that you must make an exhaustive inventory and detailed response to each question. But when a question suggests answers to your child's problems be sure to study deeper and follow the suggestions that may be implied from your own knowledge of your child.

1. *Your own recent interactions with your child.* Think about your child's history at home. What has been your relationship with your child? Have you been positive in your conversations? Have your suggestions and directions been expressed in encouraging words? Can you offer more encouragement and less criticism to good advantage? Does your child accept you as a close friend as well as a parent?

2. *Your child's attitude at home.* What about your child's attitude at home? Does your child express himself or herself in positive terms? Is your child too negative in what he or she says? Has your child been rebellious? Does your child participate in home activities and family events?

3. *How your child spends time at home.* Think about what your child does with his or her time at home. How much time has been spent in serious study and in intellectual pursuits? Are conditions around your home such that the child has good reason to be more studious? Is it hard to study in your home? Is it a frustrating place with noise and distraction?

4. *Your child's emotional condition.* Is your child generally happy? Is he or she well physically? Does your child have serious emotional problems that have developed steadily over the months without your noticing? Are there strong outbursts of temper without good reason? Is there evidence of nail chewing, bed wetting, or other manifestations of emotional trouble?

5. *Is your child active and outgoing?* Is your child outgoing in relationship to others? Does your child live largely inside of his or her own personal thoughts without expressing sincere inner thoughts and feelings? Does your child keep feelings bottled up inside? Think about the recent participation of your child in home, neighborhood, community, church, and school activities. Has your child been participating in his or her environment in a very active way or is your child very passive? Is your child shutting out activities that are needed in his or her life?

6. *Your child's friends.* Does your child have many friends? What could you conclude about your child's friends? Do your child's friends do well in school? Are they a reflection of your child and do they tend to enhance and encourage your child toward success? Would your child's friends tend to build him or her up or would the opposite be happening?

7. *Your child's recent history.* Review carefully in your mind the past year of your child's life. Then, in retrospect, think of your child's history since birth. Has the past year been filled with discouragement and frustration? Have there been some high points of accomplishment? Have there been some joyful events in

your child's life over the past year? Have any of these events occurred with you and have they been shared with the family? Have there been any events of great accomplishment and joy for your child at school? Do you believe that school activities in which your child is participating tend to add to motivation for learning and for success? Carefully concentrate on what you know about the past year's history at home, at school, with friends, in the neighborhood, and in the community insofar as your child's living is concerned. What events have been discouraging and somewhat crushing to your child? Have there been some overwhelming happenings that would give your child good reason to be discouraged and possibly want to quit trying? Remember that 80 percent of your child's learning experiences should be successful. Has this been the case or has your child experienced almost 80 percent failure? Has the past, especially the past year, been a great burden to your child? What about illnesses? What about loss of friends and difficulties in getting along with peers? Have there been any serious fights with friends or serious family fights that have been disturbing?

8. *Your child's individual identity.* Does your child have possessions of his or her own? Is there a place in your home that is unmistakably identified as the child's room or the place where the child can keep his or her possessions? Does your child have a genuine means of building true identity by having definite possessions that are his or hers that can be exclusively a part of the life of your child? Are you providing this opportunity for identity and for individuality?

9. *Your child's thoughts and aspirations.* What do you think that your child thinks about when he or she is alone? What are his or her aspirations? What are your child's interests? Is there a genuine feeling of belonging on the part of your child? Does your child feel a valued member of the family, a real part of the school, and a genuine part of community activities? Does your child have identity with groups of friends and others that would help to fill out a complete life of sharing and living with others his or her age?

10. *Your child's contributions and participation.* What organizations has your child joined? What has he or she done for others? Has your child been involved in any group projects that

will do good for others? Has your child participated in any community efforts that would better the neighborhood? Has any project been carried out that would help the poor and others that are less fortunate than you? Has your child really learned to give of himself or herself for and on behalf of others?

11. *Your child's self-discipline.* What about discipline and opportunities to learn self-control? In this age it is possible for one to live an entire lifetime without learning how to deny oneself and to discipline oneself. Through the years have you helped your child to learn the meaning of self-denial? Have you corrected with firmness but with loving care when discipline has been necessary? Does your child follow his or her impulses most of the time without restraining these desires? Does he or she do what may be expedient at the moment rather than what ought to be done? Have you truly taught your child self-control and self-discipline? Have you taught the value of hard work and the true joy of personal accomplishment? Have you kept a good balance between too much permissiveness and too much dictation and regimentation in your child's life?

12. *Your child's personal relationship to you.* Shift your thoughts and your self-questioning about your child to a deeper examination of your personal relationship. Does your child speak to you only when necessary? Does he or she merely answer your questions without taking the initiative in beginning a conversation? Does your child tell you things about himself or herself without your drawing it out through intense questioning? Who initiates most of the conversations? Does your child seem to want to get away from you as soon as possible? Do you truly believe that your child enjoys your presence and enjoys talking with you? Does your child seem to act genuine and relaxed in your presence?

13. *Your child's physical appearance and grooming.* What about your child's physical appearance? Is he or she a bit on the homely or awkward side? What about your child's clothing? Are you doing all you can to help your child look well groomed, in step with his or her peers? Do you have any reason to believe that your child might be a social misfit? Are you helping your child to emphasize the strong points of physical appearance? Does the clothing, hair style, and personal grooming of your child need more attention and care from you?

14. *Your child's intellectual life.* What about your child's intellectual diet? What does your child read? Are you providing the proper stimulation? What can you do to encourage more reading and better quality of reading? What entertainment does your child seek when a free choice is available? What types of television shows and movies are selected? That which goes into the intellectual development of a child is certainly vital. Try to determine whether your child's experiences in this regard have been positive and uplifting. The home must provide a stimulating intellectual climate if the school is to receive the kind of support that is necessary for success.

THE SELF-IMAGE

In this searching examination of your child, let's examine some questions about the child's feelings about himself or herself. The self-image is certainly a major factor in the battle for success, happiness, and identity. Many children who experience failure in school have a very poor self-image. What does your child think about herself or himself? Try to be very objective in answering this question. Be careful that you do not deceive yourself. Think about the conversations that you have had and think about the other opportunities where your close contact with your child would tell you about the self-image. Every human being must think well of himself. Strive very sincerely to gain a good assessment of your child's self-concept.

GAINING FACTS FROM YOUR CHILD'S TEACHER

It is important in your fact-finding effort to get as much information as you possibly can about your child's life at school. Much of this can come from your child's teacher or teachers. Be sure that you make appointments and spend the necessary time to get a good background on your child's life at school and your child's relationship to the teachers. Be sure to be positive in your questioning. Don't approach your child's teacher with the idea of fixing blame. You will want to help your child by soliciting the positive response of the teacher. You should convey the concept that you are concerned about your child and his or her failure in school. Make sure that your child's teacher gets a genuine impression from you that you want to be helpful and that you want to contribute to the progress of your child in school.

Try to learn about your child's basic study skills. Can your child read with sufficient skill and comprehension to gain necessary knowledge that is essential for school studies? Is your child's basic mathematics ability satisfactory? What about other basic study skills such as spelling, use of the English language, and other vital tool subjects?

In approaching your child's teacher it is important that you keep in mind that your child is just one of many that the teacher must be concerned about. Be careful about being too demanding upon the teacher, but feel free to get the information that you need. Ask your child's teacher to be totally candid with you. Be sure that you are not defensive in seeking this information. If your approach is open, you will get the kind of response that will be helpful to you.

Ask to see samples of your child's work. *Ask the teacher to describe specific instances of difficulties so that you can get a true picture of your child's performance at school and so that you can gain insight into how the teacher views your child's performance.* Ask for *specifics,* not just generalities. Ask what the child does that needs to be corrected and what the child fails to do. Get some specific suggestions from the teacher about how you and your family members can help at home.

CONSULTATION WITH THE SCHOOL COUNSELOR

In most modern school systems a counselor or a professionally trained school psychologist will be available for consultation if your child is having serious difficulties. In some schools with extremely limited budgets the specialists may not be available. In such instances, however, the principal tries to function in this capacity. If you cannot gain the assistance of a school counselor or psychologist, try to get as much of the information described below as possible from your principal.

Strive to learn if your child has normal ability. If there are serious defects or deficiencies or if your child is seriously retarded mentally, you need to have this information. If there are inherited defects that cannot be corrected, you should, of course, face these facts and then do the best that you can from there. If your child has a low IQ and has limited learning capacity, you will want to know this so that you will not expect too much and add frustration and pressure to the problem. Strive to get information about various tests that have been administered. Get information about aptitude and interest tests. Get information on standardized achievement tests that may give you some clues as to how you might help. If psychological tests have been administered, try to get a background on these. Request all possible assistance, and ask for the best estimate available as to your child's potential as well as to the possible difficulties that your child may have in learning. Get a true assessment and be willing to face the facts. But remember that there are very few children who cannot learn if you or someone else will spend the time and do those things that will motivate and touch the interest and ability level.

ASSESSING ALL THE FACTS

What do all of these facts tell you? Do you have a handicapped child? Are your child's capacities for success at school and in life within the normal range of most human beings? If there are no apparent physical or mental defects, you should be ready to think through a course of action to improve the school performance of your child. In most cases of school failure the child has emotional and attitudinal problems or problems of motivation and commitment. Incidents of mental and physical handicap, of course, will need special assistance from trained professionals. But most of the cases of school failure can be largely remedied by careful cooperation between home and the school.

THE GREAT POTENTIAL OF THE HOME

What are the obstacles and problems that you, the child, and the school can correct? As you seek to answer this question, assessing the facts that you have gathered, remember that the home has the greatest impact upon the child. Possibly you as the parent have the greatest potential and also the greatest responsibility for helping your child find his or her way to success. This is not to say that a heavy responsibility is not shared by the school. But with large numbers of children the opportunity for in-depth individualized assistance is more limited at school as compared to the home. With your love, concern, and emotional affiliation with your child the opportunity for genuinely effective assistance on a continuous basis over a long period of time must be seized upon by you and by other members of your family.

In your interviews at school with the teacher, the counselor, the school psychologist, and others, have you learned some new facts? If so, are you willing to accept them? Are you being realistic and objective in your assessment of these facts? Beware of your own tendency to obscure the facts or to alibi around them. We are so emotionally involved in our children's lives that we can very easily find ourselves lacking in objectivity and the ability to face the facts. You must define the problems, accept your share of the blame (if there is any to share) and recognize the problems for what they are. Many parents refuse to do this. They blame the school, the child, the child's friends, the church, or the neighborhood. But they don't see themselves and see the problems that are generated in the home that may really be the root of the child's difficulties. This is not to say that the school cannot and should not share the blame. We all know of situations where incompetent teachers and unfortunate school practices contribute to the difficulties of children at school. But you should keep in mind that the great majority of children do quite well at school and that most of the difficulties in learning can be corrected by parents willing to approach the problem intelligently and face the facts with true determination and commitment to see that difficulties are eradicated.

Remember, the first step in solving any problem is to recognize that you have one. Recognize that the facts surrounding the problems of your child and his or her learning difficulties are very real. If you have thought through all the questions and have studied the school situation with some care, you should come to this point in your campaign to help your child succeed with great insight and knowledge. Your goal from this point will be to help your child realize more fully his or her total potential.

PLANNING A WISE AND INSIGHTFUL COURSE OF ACTION

The words *wise* and *insightful* in the above heading are very significant. Remember that you are a long way down the road to real success for your child if you have done a thorough job of thinking about the most critical problems and if you have accepted them objectively and realistically. But you must proceed with wisdom and care from this point.

WORKING WITH THE TEACHER

After you have appraised the problems and obstacles to success at school, be sure to talk to your child's teacher or teachers. Enlist the teacher's special interest and support. Set up a means of continuous communication. Strive to arrive at some mutual conclusions and understandings. Both you and the child's teacher should be working in close cooperation to help your child down the road toward success. Neither you nor the school can do this alone. Be sure to ask for suggestions and for reactions to your conclusions. Offer some of your own suggestions and raise questions that you think might be relevant to the situation. (In all of this, remember that your child is one of many children at school. Teachers have heavy work loads and there is a limit to what you can expect to be done for your child as one individual among hundreds.) Be sure that you have established a means of keeping in touch with your child's teacher. Constant communication will be vital from this point on.

REMOVING OBSTACLES AT HOME

Try to analyze the problems and obstacles that may have been caused by you and by your family. Remember that if you have contributed to the lack of success you can also remove these obstacles and enhance the opportunities for learning. If you do find that you share a large part of the blame for the child's learning problems, you should not be unduly guilt-ridden about this. All parents make mistakes. The important point now is to correct them. Resolve to do all that you can to convert the information you have gained to good use. Most of all, resolve to change your home to become a much more powerful and supportive influence over the child's life and learning opportunities. Following are points to serve as a check list as you proceed to change the home influence and impact on your child:

1. If you find that your child needs more study time at home, set up the most pleasant conditions and surroundings possible for this.

2. If you find that your child has met with too much failure, try to establish circumstances and encourage your child to work on a level where success will be highly probable. In all of this, be careful that your actions are wise and appropriate.

3. Don't add to the frustrations and don't, in your eagerness, overpower your child with attention, pressure, and demands.

4. Establish better and more meaningful communication with your child. If your conversation has not contributed to the child's outlook, be sure that you change your mode and emphasis of conversation.

5. Set up successful, reinforcing experiences that are genuine—not contrived—but that will result in *real* successes.

6. You may find that you need to make quite a dramatic change in your child's intellectual diet and overall stimulation and exposure. If this is necessary, be sure that you proceed in a gradual and carefully planned approach.

7. Use your child's interest to provide good reading.

8. Encourage as much as possible and demand as little as possible so that you will not generate resentment and anger. This can be done if you strive to make the conditions genuinely satisfactory from the child's point of view.

9. Look for opportunities to give praise that is sincerely meant.

10. Try to get much closer to your child by sharing experiences and by building a natural desire for conversation that draws the child out and leaves much of the listening to you. Keep in mind, though, that a phony new approach that suddenly showers the child with attention may do a great deal of harm and may shut the child off from you.

11. Set up a new means of listening to your child and a new approach to exploring and sharing common interests.

12. If you will express your true inner feelings and

concerns in a genuine and loving way, the chances are that you will succeed in getting to your child's true nature where his or her aspirations and fears will be expressed.

NEED FOR POSITIVE OUTLOOK

All of this may be a very long journey if your child is somewhat disturbed and if you have not had a close relationship in the past. But if you approach this effort in a very sincere manner with true love and concern, the progress might be surprisingly encouraging. Be strong on positive encouragement and be very cautious with correction and negative response. It is not possible, nor even wise, of course, to be positive and complimentary at all times. But you must avoid the negative, the constant correction that is so prevalent between many parents and children. It is important to place special emphasis on this point because we often find a negative and nagging approach almost universally attached to a failing and frustrated child.

THE CHILD'S PHYSICAL WELL-BEING

In your program of corrective action and building of new relationships, be sure not to neglect the child's physical appearance and well-being. Good nutrition, wholesome exercise, plenty of rest, and a pleasing physical appearance with nice clothes and well-groomed hair will do much for the failing child. In a gradual program of improvement, try to lead your child to higher standards of physical health, personal appearance, and grooming. There is a close relationship between these factors and learning, and all of this is tied to self-concept and positive self-image. Be sure not to neglect these vital aspects.

GOALS AND RECOGNITION

When you have reached the point of improving your rapport with your child and improving the self-image and physical appearance and health, you will be ready to lead your child very carefully to some goal setting to improve school performance in a very direct way. Try to get the child to accept a reasonable program of home-based study. Do this in close cooperation with the school. Know what the academic needs are at school and fill as many of these as possible at home. Try to do this without exercising dictatorial demands over the child, but rather with a careful approach, preparing the way with genuine love and understanding. First you must have established a new relationship and an emotional closeness to your child. Use the child's special interests and aptitudes where possible. Use friends and peer group help if this is feasible and wise. Gradually and systematically bring the child's study skills and commitments to learning along. Be sure that the child experiences more success than failure. In all of this it is, of course, important to solicit assistance from the school and to make sure that your efforts and the efforts at school move along hand in hand in close cooperation.

AVOIDING DISCOURAGEMENT

Many disturbed and failing students have a stormy recovery period. You should not expect the road to be smooth and easy. There will likely be relapses and periods of great discouragement.

The keys to success at this point are perseverance and constant communication with the school. It is difficult to do, but you should try to devote a great amount of time to creating a new climate, a new personal relationship, and a new set of positive circumstances. This will require genuine awareness of your role and a strong personal commitment from you.

The heartaches of raising a failing child are many. The rewards are well worth the effort. When you show both the child and the school that you care, that you will go to great lengths and expend considerable energy and sacrifice for success, the response is usually positive and rewarding. But you must keep in touch with the specifics. All the facts described in this chapter must be kept current. There must be full commitment on your part. A child in trouble is an enormous challenge for both the home and the school. There is no magic road back to the normal channels of behavior and successful performance. But if you are willing to get the facts, to assess them accurately, and to follow a course of action suggested in this chapter, you will have a great chance for success.

WHEN TO GET PROFESSIONAL HELP

If your child is behind several grade levels in academic

accomplishment and if he or she has been having basic study skill deficiencies in areas such as reading and mathematics, you may have some serious psychological problems. It may be that your child is so seriously disturbed emotionally that you will need special help from the school. You may even need to seek professional psychiatric assistance from outside of the school. Be sure to assess this carefully and make the sacrifice to get this assistance. You should not shrink from asking for special help from the school district if you find that your problems are beyond your means and capacity for solution.

Most school systems have specially trained remedial teachers. They have school psychologists, social workers, and diagnostic personnel. If your problem is truly beyond the scope of your own resources, then you should seek assistance and avail yourself of the special services available in your school system. The school principal will know of these special services and will be willing to help you obtain them.

THE CHALLENGE AND REWARD

The challenge of being a parent in a family of normal and well-adjusted children can be frustrating and discouraging at times. But the challenge of leading a child back to success when he or she has experienced serious failure is indeed a great opportunity as well as a source of considerable frustration. Too many parents give up too easily. If your child is failing at school, or is doing only average work when there is obvious capacity for superior accomplishment, you should meet this problem with total confidence and full commitment.

As you review all the details of this chapter you may feel overwhelmed with all that has been suggested. But remember that you do not have to do everything that is suggested because your child will most likely not have anywhere near the total number of problems covered in the discussion. Take a few items and do what you can. Remember that the total range of suggestions extend beyond what will be necessary for your child, unless the difficulties are unusually extensive.

9.
A Final Message

Successful parents must be actively concerned about the education of their children. But this concern does not present an added burden so much as it does a new style of living and learning with your children. *As you teach incidentally as a natural outgrowth of your day-to-day interaction with your children, you merely need to think actively about the fact that you are indeed a very powerful teacher as well as a parent.* By being continuously involved with the learning activities of your children you will stay young in mind and spirit. So do not be overwhelmed with the task. Remember that you do not have to apply every detail suggested in this book nor carry out every item of direction to the letter. Just become fully conscious of your role as the most influential teacher your children will ever have. Be relaxed and confident that you can make a big difference in your child's intellectual growth. Remember that this can be done just by offering love that is genuine and help that is given with common sense and with a full awareness that it takes neither perfection nor genius to help your child excel in school.

Most of parenting is simply the application of good common sense. Fortunately, the responsibility of parenting does not have to be carried alone. Much help is available through the schools and through other agencies. Through application of some simple common sense measures and through constant close contact with those who can be of assistance, the burden of parenting can be greatly lightened.

Remember the importance of self-concept and its relationship to school achievement. Try to help your child to be confident and to think well of himself or herself. This is so vital that it merits repetition here. Find a child who is troubled at school and you will almost always find a child who lacks confidence and has a very poor self-concept. Conversely, find a child who is doing well in school and you will find a child filled with self-confidence and imbued with the feeling that he or she is just about as happy and capable as the other person.

To summarize some of the vital points in this book: Two fundamental skills should be established during the earliest possible years in your child's lifetime. These are (1) the ability to communicate and use vocabulary effectively, and (2) the ability to utilize arithmetic reasoning and number concepts easily and fluently. Be sure to help your child build vocabulary power in the home. Help your child in self expression, in listening skills, and in the vital capacity to communicate and express thoughts. Your conversation can build and maintain mental alertness and mental power if you will help build high-level mind-stretching communication through keeping the same constantly flowing in your home. Word power is, to a considerable extent, mental power. Mathematics is, of course, almost pure logic. Much attention must be given to these capabilities.

Remember that active minds are growing all through the public school years. Provide a high level of mental stimulation for your child. Be sure to provide high-quality, provocative thoughts to your children through conversation that is on their interest levels and that is constantly broadening the frontiers of their thinking.

Keep your child *active and involved* in community activities, school affairs, and church social programs. Seek activities that will help to build your child's social skills. Activities are very important in the educational lives of your children. Such participation will bring variety and balance into their lives. You will want to build a high level of social competence and social intelligence, and will want to help your children develop outgoing, participating personalities. Keep the concept in mind that activities do more than entertain. By encouraging your children to participate in activities, you will help to attain these important goals and you will be rewarded with children who will grow healthy personalities and will gradually mature into well-rounded young adults.

Another key thought from this book that is worth further emphasis is the concept that you should strive to make your home an educational center. Always be thinking in terms of education as you relate to your children. Provide books, encourage much reading, and have stimulating discussions about things that are read. Enrich the lives of your children at home with music, art, and fine literature. Your home must be a teaching-learning place. Life at home must be varied and stimulating. Your home must change, of course, as your children grow in language capacity and in mental abilities. This may sound like a job beyond your capacity but you should remember that it does not all have to be done in one day or even in one year. The long and steady process of reaching maturity should be matched with a gradual transition so that you advance the quality and the quantity of the learning experiences as your children advance. Don't let your home become a stagnant place. Keep a constant flow of books, periodicals, and newspapers before your children. Encourage reading and foster stimulating, mind-stretching conversation that will keep your children reading and studying all through their growing years. Your home must be a place for study and contemplation as well as a place for activity and stimulation. Provide a place that encourages study. Make your entire residence a place that challenges the mind to be alert, active, and dynamic in its growth. *Remember that your home can greatly compensate for deficiencies that may occur other places in the life of your child. But it is very difficult for any individual or institution to compensate for failure in the home.*

Economic literacy and career education must be emphasized in your home. Your children must gradually grow to a point where they can earn a place in the economic system of our society. Therefore you have a responsibility constantly to help your children learn about the value of work and the worth and dignity of many careers. You must be thinking career education in your home and you must be teaching about our society, which is both productive and competitive. Expose your children to many career opportunities. Provide interest-building experiences that will lead to wise career choices. Help to build career competence and help your children to utilize the school system as a means to success in this vital field. Teach the value of money and the great worth of the habit of thrift and conservation of financial resources. If you pay proper attention to the responsibilities of offering economics and career education in the home, you will help to build those qualities in your children that will make transition into adulthood easy, rewarding, and enjoyable. All of this you may do slowly and steadily each month as you think and talk with your child. Your career counseling activity can be low key and relaxed. So don't be discouraged or think the task is beyond your capacity.

The admonition to keep close to your children's school is worthy of further emphasis in this summary. Think of the school as a resource. Use the services at school. Know the curriculum and help your child to master it and gain the greatest amount possible from it. Know the teachers and make a special effort to get to know the administrators and other special services personnel. Know about school affairs and school activities. Be cognizant of the problems at school and offer your support so that your neighborhood school will always be an active and dynamic institution for your children. Help build quality in your school by being close to it and by offering a positive, supportive hand when needed.

Be positively critical of your child's school when necessary. Be sure to call often and keep in touch so the regrets will be few and the lost opportunities will be limited. *Never forget that parenting of school age children requires constant contact with teachers, counselors, school principals, and school district officials.* Communication with the school should be accompanied with a "how-can-I-help attitude."

Remember that the schools can't do the job alone. Parents need to know what the school program is and support and supplement it in the home. You can't do this without keeping in touch with the child's teachers and without knowing where encouragement and assistance will be needed during critical times in the child's learning career. So keep in touch and be responsive. This requires continuous, active parent concern.

Another point of further emphasis in this summary is to remember the spiritual, the ideal, and the road to true God-like conduct for your children. Insist on clean speech, reverent conduct, spirituality, and a love and respect for all life. Avoid bigotry and prejudice in your home and avoid it in any example that your children might see or hear from you. If you follow this road yourself, you will lead the way for your children. Be active in the church of your choice, but don't send your children to church—take them with you to church. Reach for those values that transcend the ordinary and your children will be on the way to rich and rewarding lives. Encourage the inspiration of the arts and humanities to become a part of your home and a part of the life of your children. Help your children to seek the so-called good things of life through fine music, great art, and enjoyment of nature's wonders. Remember the spiritual and aesthetic aspects of life during those few years that you will have your children in your home growing and living and learning with you.

It is important to emphasize again in this summary that you should watch for the critical points and the crisis events as your children grow up. Know when a stormy period is coming and help your child to weather the crisis. There are many crises that come along during the growing period of a person's life. Be alert to help. Know when troubles are small and have the good sense to stay away so your child can grow from the lessons of mild adversity. Adversity helps to shape character. If you take all adversity out of your child's life you deprive the child, even though you intend to be helpful. It takes a wise parent to know when to permit the child to "go it alone." On the other hand, you should know the symptoms of serious trouble and seek the help of others before it is too late.

Parents should strike a good balance between too much domination and control and excessive freedom and permissiveness. Be an advocate, a parent counselor, and a rock of stability to your children. *But don't dictate. Domineering parents are as harmful as overly permissive parents.* Seek the golden mean between doing too much and too little. Strike a good balance between trying to raise your children in your exact image and offering no control or direction. Know the difference between leading and pushing. Know the difference between encouraging and directing. Adjust your touch and your style to the unique needs of each child in your family. One child may need a great deal more guidance and assistance than another. Be alert to these individual differences and adapt your style and your approach accordingly.

Additional emphasis should be placed upon the need to make reasonable demands and to set attainable standards of performance for your children. *Remember that discipline can be very instructive if it is utilized properly. Discipline is like mild forms of adversity in its role in helping to shape character. The keys to good discipline are consistency, compassion, and gentle loving firmness. Don't vacillate with your rules and standards.* Children like fair, even, reasonable rules so that they know what to expect.

Here again, common sense and consideration of human relations will guide you considerably. Remember that it will be harmful to your children to grow up in a home where rules and standards of performance are missing. It will be harmful to them to grow up thinking that parents are servants and that very little work needs to be performed around the home. Have duties and reasonable work loads for your children and have some sensible rules that will teach the great truth that real joy and fulfillment come from honest work and accepting of responsibility. Many parents fail in applying these principles, not because they do not want to do everything possible for their children but because they strive to do everything possible. Examine your behavior insofar as your standards, discipline, and assignment of work responsibilities are concerned. Don't deprive your children of the opportunities implicit in reasonable demands and attainable standards of performance.

Possibly the greatest joy in life is the joy of accomplishment through expenditure of one's own efforts to reach an important goal. Help your children to be goal directed. Plan with them and find the pleasure of parenting that comes with seeing your own children succeed. Hard work that is accepted with a willing heart should be one of the major family aims. What your children really need in life is work. Teach your children to carry a fair share of the work load around the home and the neighborhood. This is good parenting at its best. Parents should not, of course, exploit children by making excessive demands. By example we must show that we are willing to do our own fair share and to go more than the second mile with the child. But as the child is capable of doing so, make sure that he or she carries the full share of the work. To do otherwise is actually to be cruel to your children, for they will learn some hard lessons in later life that you failed to teach them at home when it was easy for them to learn.

Don't be so practical and pragmatic that you forget to play and share in a few of the light and fun things of life. Plan outings, vacations, weekends, and evenings that are spent for the sole purpose of having a good time together as a family. These activities will strengthen your influence and power to lead your children. They will give you insights into how you can be a better parent counselor. They will tie your family together by creating experiences that are memorable to all of the family and will become part of the family history in later years.

YOUR INTERPERSONAL RELATIONSHIPS WITH YOUR CHILDREN

The greatest teaching power for parents comes through love that is unfeigned and supportive. This provides the mortar that will hold you together as a family. Love is possibly the greatest motivating power, the greatest holding power, and the greatest path to family unity. Show your children that you love them by expressing it in a genuine, wholesome, and natural way.

In this connection, you need to have long and earnest conversations with each child on an individual and very personal basis. These conversations must be regular. They must truly touch the heart of the child, and the conversations must come from your heart if they are going to do this.

Eminently successful parents—parents with great power to guide children—have a special relationship with their children. They let each child know that they *care*. They let each child know that they will go to any lengths to help. They let each child know that they are fair, reasonable, and lovingly sympathetic.

THE BURDEN IS LIGHT — ENJOY IT!

Take the time that is needed with your family. Devote yourself to your children and you will be rewarded by the joys of seeing their success and happiness. Helping your child through your active concern for his or her full and complete education is a long but delightful course. There is also no joy like that of rejoicing in the success and happiness of your own child.

As you apply the principles espoused in this book, do not be overwhelmed with the detail nor regard the challenge as being beyond your capacity. Be *actively concerned* with your child's education and make your contribution in the natural setting of your home. You will find that the burden is light and that the rewards are well worth the effort. *All it actually requires is active parent concern and a few additional minutes each day.*

APPENDICES

INTRODUCTION TO APPENDICES A AND B

The discussion that follows will be useful to those readers interested in getting involved more deeply in the affairs of school governance. The material in Appendix A will help you to understand the system of governing public schools in the United States. The roles of state legislators, governors, state departments of education, the local school board, and the superintendent of schools are described. The recent influence of the judicial system upon education affairs will be of interest to some readers. Since school taxes and the financing of schools are matters of concern to many parents, this topic is also treated in Appendix A.

In recent years the education associations and teachers' unions have been actively involved in collective bargaining with school boards. This activity and resultant strikes by teacher organizations, and the impact of the same on the schools, may be of interest to some parents. These topics are also discussed in Appendix A.

APPENDICES

In Appendix B will be found information about parent teacher associations, how they are organized on the local level and how parents may become more actively involved. Since local school boards make many decisions that influence children and matters related to the schools, many parents will want to learn more about how to work with school board members. Information on this topic is also presented in Appendix B.

Appendix A
The School and the School System Bureaucracy

When our system of government was established by the founding fathers, the matter of education was delegated to the states. It was the belief of most of the leaders who established our Constitution that education should remain close to the people and that the control and finance of education should remain on the grass-roots level.

Each state has its own provisions for education. Every state constitution emphasizes the importance of education and accepts responsibility for support and maintenance of a public school system. The laws and the system of governance of education are broadly diverse. But in this diversity are many common threads.

Your child's school is a member unit in a large family of schools that make up a total school system. The basic unit for governing education in almost every state is the school district. Most school districts are actually locally chartered units of state government. The chief policy-making body for these school districts is the state legislature. In most states these school districts are independent from control of the mayor, the governor, the county commissioner, etc. Because of this, you have great responsibility to vote in school elections and to help school systems to be responsive to the people.

THE STATE LEGISLATURE AND YOUR SCHOOL

In most of the states of the United States the state legislature has passed laws that provide for financial support of schools. The state lawmaking bodies have also provided for the system of governance of the local school district. In almost every state a local board of education has been given the responsibility by the state legislature to govern the schools, to levy taxes, and to promulgate rules and regulations under which public schools will operate. The authority of these local boards of education has been prescribed by laws passed by the state legislature. The amount of money and the limits to taxes are all set by the state legislature. A total body of school law has been enacted in most states and this group of laws has a profound impact upon the educational opportunities for your children and for your neighbors' children.

Your state legislature and the state representatives and senators elected by you and your neighbors determine to a very great extent the powers, restrictions, and provisions for education. You should be actively concerned about the views of state legislators and candidates for state legislature as related to public education.

THE GOVERNOR AND YOUR SCHOOL

The chief executive officer of the state is, of course, the governor. The governors prepare the annual or biennial budgets which include provisions for support of education. Most governors, in their regular messages to state legislatures, recommend changes in the levels of finance and in the legal provisions for public schools. With this power to recommend changes and to initiate budget levels, the governor of your state has a profound impact upon your school. Add to this the enormous power of the veto, and you can see that the governor is a very influential person insofar as education is concerned. You should be deeply concerned about the views of persons who are candidates for the high office of governor in your state. You should be active in gubernatorial politics and you should express your views concerning the recommendations that your governor makes about education.

THE STATE DEPARTMENT OF EDUCATION AND YOUR SCHOOL

One of the most important departments in state government is the State Department of Education. The implementation of laws enacted by the legislature is delegated to the State Department of Education. Most State Departments of Education are governed by a State Board of Education. Usually the State Board of Education is either appointed by the governor or elected by popular ballot. This State Board promulgates regulations and carries out certain regulatory responsibilities delegated to it by the legislature.

The State Department of Education is headed by a chief state school officer with the title of Commissioner of Education or State Superintendent of Public Instruction. (Other titles such as Secretary of Education are sometimes used.) This officer works under the direction of the State Board of Education and serves as the head of the State Department of Public Instruction. The authority of the State Department of Education over your local school comes only through the school district. But through this authority standards, rules, and state-level guidelines are set. These are very important to you and to your neighbors.

Most State Departments of Education are responsible for licensing teachers and school administrators. State Boards of Education adopt rules and regulations concerning the educational background and other qualifications for teaching and for entering into school administration. Some State Departments of Education have authority delegated to them by the legislature to develop curriculum standards and to promulgate regulations that control graduation requirements. A few State Departments of Education have responsibility for adopting textbooks and for approving the instructional materials used by local school districts. This is not the case, however, in most of the states.

The State Board of Education, the chief state school officer, and the professional staff members in the State Department of Public Instruction provide leadership and carry out regulatory responsibilities as prescribed by the state legislature. As these responsibilities are assumed on the state level, the individuals holding these offices make decisions and perform services that have an impact upon the quality of education that your child receives.

THE COURTS AND YOUR CHILD'S SCHOOL

The state and federal courts are becoming increasingly influential in determining policies and in interpreting laws that have an impact upon your child's school. The impact of state and federal judges upon education has been increasingly important in recent years.

The courts have been adjudicating issues related to equality of opportunity. Efforts to desegregate schools and to eliminate racial isolation have been initiated by decisions handed down by the courts. The explosive issue of busing and attaining racial balance is determined by the judicial branch of government. Student rights and responsibilities, authority to enforce dress standards, authority of school officials versus authority of parents in regulating the lives of children are all being determined by the judicial branch of our government. Parents should be aware of the federal civil rights act. This law guarantees equal rights regardless of race, creed, or religion. Because racially isolated schools of ethnic minorities have been inferior in the past, the courts have ruled that they do not provide equal opportunities. Buses have been used to transport minority children to largely white schools. This has caused great controversy and apprehension. Continued litigation in the courts is to be expected before the issue is settled.

Parents should be aware of the great impact that the courts and the judicial system are having upon education in America. As human rights and equality have become matters of public concern, the judges on the state and federal levels have been and will continue to hand down decisions that will have a profound effect upon public education.

THE LOCAL BOARD OF EDUCATION

Of all governing bodies, the local board of education carries the weight of many decisions that daily touch the lives of your child and his or her education. Most local school boards are elected by the public. In a few states the local school board is appointed either by the governor or by the Board of County Commissioners or Board of County Supervisors. These board of education members are elected or appointed to serve you and to serve the educational needs of your child.

The local school board member has specific responsibilities prescribed by the school laws and by the state legislature. Some regulations promulgated by the State Board of Education and State Department of Education govern the activities of the local school board. In most states the power of the local board of education is enormous. Broad discretionary authority and responsibility to make far-reaching educational decisions rest in the hands of the local board of education.

The local board of education employs the superintendent of schools. Upon recommendation of the superintendent of schools, other staff members including the principal and the teachers in your local school are hired by the local board of education. Perhaps one of the most important functions of the local school board is the selection and employment of the chief executive officer for your school district, the superintendent of schools. The nature of this selection of a superintendent will have a profound impact upon the quality of education in your school district.

Your local board of education usually has power to levy taxes upon local property and to adopt budgets for schools. Salary schedules for employees of the school district and requirements for employment are adopted by the local board of education. Local regulations on attendance, assignment of students to various schools, establishment of school bus routes, selection of textbooks and instructional materials are all ultimately the responsibility of the local board of education and the superintendent of schools. The construction of school buildings, the opening and closing of schools, regulations for the discipline and control of students all rest in the hands of the local board of education.

Local school boards have some authority over curriculum and what is taught in the schools but they do not have a total voice in this matter. Some courses of instruction are set by law. Others are set by State Board of Education regulation. Teachers, of course, have (within limits of school board rules and the law) at least some discretion over what is taught and how much it is emphasized.

Most actions of local boards of education are taken at

school board meetings which are held in public. Citizens have the right to come before the local board of education to make recommendations, to protest actions that have been taken, and to express views concerning the organization and governance of the local schools. School board meetings are usually set in advance and are held regularly at the school district headquarters. Parents should take an active interest in these meetings and should express themselves to local school board members on issues that come before the board.

Your local school board often has very difficult choices to make. For example, regulations have to be established concerning school bus routes. This involves the roads and streets down which school buses will travel. It also involves the walking distance to school and the distance from school at which students are entitled to ride the bus. It is only natural for parents to want the school bus to stop in front of their residences. It is difficult to set the mileage distance for school transportation services. As these decisions and cutoff points are set some parents become concerned.

There is practically nothing more controversial than decisions that affect the lives of our children. An action to change a school attendance boundary may demand that your child shift from one school to another. With declining or increasing enrollments, the alteration of school attendance boundaries is often a very necessary decision. As these decisions are made by the local board of education, the lives of children and the family lives are affected. Decisions to build new schools and decisions as to where such schools should be located become matters of intense interest and controversy to parents. The local school board member must sit in public meeting and vote to the best of his or her judgment on many of these issues.

As parents take an active interest in local school district matters, they should also strive to see the problems of the total school system. Local school board members should be encouraged to make fair and equitable decisions. Parents should lend support that will keep special-interest and high-pressure groups from dominating the actions of the local school board. Parents should remember that the system of governing schools was established to keep the management of the schools close to the people by having your neighbors and fellow citizens serving as local school board members. The opportunity to influence decisions and to express views and have desires responded to will be preserved only to the extent that you are active in school board matters and well informed on school issues. You should get involved and help make grass-roots control of education work effectively. Parents should see that persons of good judgment and high personal standards are elected to the local school board. As you contemplate this brief description of the power and authority of the local board, the necessity for selecting and supporting distinguished citizens for the school board should be apparent. Many authorities are concerned about citizen apathy in school board matters. Grass-roots control of your child's school gives you a voice in educational policy. You must be active and you must be well informed if our system is to grow to meet the needs of today's world.

THE SUPERINTENDENT OF SCHOOLS

The chief educational leader in the school system is the superintendent of schools. This person is selected and employed by the board of education to be the executive officer of the school system. Under the direction of the superintendent, the principals, teachers, counselors, and other school employees carry out their responsibilities. The superintendent of schools must execute the policy and directives of the local school board. The superintendent usually makes recommendations to the board of education, prepares the agenda for board meetings, drafts initial proposals for budget making, and generally performs the functions of chief administrative officer for the board of education and for the school district.

As the chief executive officer and leader of the professional staff, the superintendent usually has a great opportunity to persuade and influence board policy. The superintendent must, of course, recommend action and be active in helping the board to settle issues and problems. In this role he or she has great influence on future direction in the school system.

In most school systems the superintendent of schools is expected to recommend the appointment of school principals. Your school principal works directly under the management and supervision of the superintendent or of a high-level official on the superintendent's staff. In smaller school systems the superintendent is able to work directly and personally with the principal of each school. In very large school systems, however, other administrative staff members such as an area superintendent or an assistant superintendent carry out the responsibility of directing and supervising the work of the local school principal. But in all circumstances, the superintendent of schools is responsible to the board of education for policies that are adopted by the board. Many of the administrative decisions of the superintendent touch the daily school life of your child.

The superintendent of schools must understand education and the total school curriculum. He or she must be an instructional leader with high commitment to the ideals and purposes of educating children. The level of excellence and the total commitment to true quality in education begins with the quality of leadership provided by the superintendent.

The superintendent must understand school finance and business management. He or she must have expertise in human relations and in communications. The superintendent must be a dynamic leader with ability to generate loyalty and total staff commitment to a quality program of education. The superintendent must have the ability to speak in public meetings and explain and gain support for the educational program of the school system.

Under the direction of the superintendent of schools, money, supplies, and materials are allocated to the schools. After the board of education adopts the school district budget, the superintendent of schools makes administrative decisions in allocating money and materials to the various schools on an equitable basis that should provide equality of educational opportunity throughout the school system. The maintenance of school buildings, the management of a transportation system, the administration of the school curriculum, and the standards of the district all emanate from the quality of leadership of the superintendent of schools and his central administrative staff.

Most school districts employ supervisors and curriculum specialists to work with principals and teachers in areas of specialty essential to education. Some special educational programs such as vocational education, education for handicapped children, and education of low-income and minority children require special administrative staff members on the district headquarters level. State and federal red tape and the meeting of regulations and requirements prescribed by law occupy a considerable amount of time of the district headquarters staff. All of these functions must be articulated by the superintendent of schools in a manner that will result in optimum learning opportunities for children.

FINANCING THE PUBLIC SCHOOLS

In most states the financing of public education is shared by state and local taxes with a relatively lesser amount of money coming from the federal government. The power to levy taxes on local property for school purposes is usually delegated to the board of education. In most states the board of education is limited in the amount of tax that can be levied on the local level.

In most of the states the state legislature appropriates money for schools from state taxes. The most common sources of funds are property, income, and sales taxes. Usually the state legislature provides a level of support in a school foundation program that guarantees a minimum amount of money for the education of each child. In most school finance formulas the local school board is required to levy a tax that is then matched on a formula basis with state money to provide the guaranteed amount per child. Unfortunately, many states have very poor equalization programs. In many school districts the amount of money available for support of the education of children is determined by the property tax wealth of the district. There are enormous inequities in some states. It is not uncommon to find one school system with almost twice as much money per child for education as a neighboring district in the state. Recent progress and public attention have been focused on these inequities through lawsuits and through citizen pressure for more fairness and equity in school financing.

The maximum amount of money that can be raised by your local school board for education of your children and your neighbors' children is determined by the state legislature and by the school finance laws. Each time the legislature meets, this level of support is fixed by laws that appropriate state money and delegate authority to local school boards concerning local taxing powers. After the legislature has acted on these matters of financing schools, the local board of education and the superintendent of schools are able to utilize a school finance formula in calculating the amount of revenue available.

After the revenue has been calculated, budgets are drawn up that allocate money to the various categories in the school system budget. The age-old problem of priorities comes into the picture during budgeting time—deciding which purposes are worthier of money than others. Most states require local boards of education to hold a budget hearing before they adopt the budget.

This provides an opportunity for citizens to come before the board of education and express views concerning the school budget and the educational priorities reflected in the budget.

Parents interested in adequate schooling for their children should be active in seeing that there is adequate financial support. Education should be a high priority for your taxes. You should be informed about school finances, and you should know how your school tax dollars are spent—what priorities are set and what educational results are purchased. Most states have laws that require public hearings on school district budgets. But these are usually poorly attended. Parents should become much more active in the entire matter of financing schools and allocating dollars to sound priorities.

In most states money for construction of school buildings and for building the capital assets of a school system comes from a different taxing authority than does money for the ongoing operation of the school. Most schools have a provision for issuing bonds and paying for school buildings on a long-term basis where revenue over a period of years makes a major purchase of a school building. This is not unlike the process of a family's financing a purchase whereby income is committed over a period of years to make a major purchase of a capital asset.

School finance is a source of great controversy in most states. Debates in legislative halls are generated from various pressure groups desiring to shift the tax burden from one place to another. The level of school finance and particularly the level of teacher salaries enter into the issues. By becoming knowledgeable about the local school district budget and by being informed about the state school finance formula parents can more effectively influence decisions made by the legislature and by local school boards.

EDUCATION ASSOCIATIONS AND TEACHERS' UNIONS

Like other segments of our society, teachers in recent years have been organizing to advance the level of salaries, fringe benefits, and other economic matters. Collective bargaining between teachers and school boards is quite common. There have been a few statewide teacher strikes and numerous strikes on the local school district level.

Two major national organizations, the National Education

Association and the American Federation of Teachers, have been leading teacher groups to utilize the collective strength of teachers to advance the economic well-being of persons engaged in the teaching profession. State and local organizations usually affiliate with one of these two national groups. There has been some action recently to bring about a unification of the two teachers' organizations. The National Education Association is not affiliated with labor unions whereas the American Federation of Teachers is an affiliate of the huge AFL-CIO organization. Most teachers belong to organizations affiliated with the National Education Association; however the American Federation of Teachers has been gaining in membership, particularly in the large urban centers of the country.

Local and state teacher organizations send delegates to national conventions where the business of these national organizations is transacted. Goals are set and efforts are made to seek objectives that have been determined from these national conventions. The national organizations assist the locals when they are in trouble. Advice and technical assistance are given when collective bargaining efforts are under way. Teachers are offered insurance benefits, investment opportunities, and other advantages that come from affiliation with a huge national organization.

Most likely, the teachers in your school are affiliated with one of these two national organizations. It is also highly probable that these teachers belong to the school district's education association or the school district level unit of the American Federation of Teachers. Some teachers in your neighborhood school may be officers in the organization on the local and/or state levels.

Most boards of education enter into collective bargaining agreements with teacher organizations. Annual collective bargaining for salaries and fringe benefits is quite common, although many school districts are now entering into multi-year contracts quite similar to those found in industry. Collective bargaining has been expanding to include matters other than fringe benefits. Teacher working conditions such as class size and number of hours spent in actual instruction have been subjects of tense bargaining in recent years. The principal of your neighborhood school and the superintendent of schools in your local school district have the responsibility of working with the organized teaching profession and executing the terms of negotiated agreements worked out between the board and the teachers' organization. In recent years the collective action of teachers has generated a certain amount of tension between administrators and teacher groups. As collective bargaining becomes more uniformly accepted and as both management and teacher groups gain more sophistication in the bargaining process, the overtones of stress and adversity will likely be ameliorated. Most of the states have teacher bargaining laws and the rules for bargaining have been fairly well established. However, in many states there are no laws governing collective bargaining between school boards and teachers.

Many school policies are being decided through the collective bargaining process. The voice of the parent is not often heard. More parental attention must be brought into the collective bargaining process. How this is done in the future might well determine the future of grass-roots control of our schools. This may well be one of the most critical issues on the current scene in education.

Some observers on the educational scene complain that the quality of education will be damaged as collective bargaining becomes more established. Others, however, believe that the opposite will happen and that students as well as teachers will benefit from the collective bargaining movement that is in full sway across the country. This will likely be true if you and many parents get involved in this issue, participate in the rule making, and see that parents' views are heeded. Whether you are against strikes or believe they are a basic right of teachers, your views should be heard. Many accept the point of view that teachers have a right to bargain collectively for economic benefits and that even strikes are justified in unusual circumstances. Collective bargaining for public employees such as teachers, policemen, firemen, and other governmental workers is still evolving across the country. As this movement develops further and as government has experience in coping with collective measures of employee groups, there will likely be more legislation passed on the state and national level.

THE FEDERAL GOVERNMENT AND YOUR NEIGHBORHOOD SCHOOL

Money allocated for support of the schools comes from from state and local sources. Since 1965 the United States Congress has appropriated large sums of money for allocation to local school districts. The largest amount of money appropriated from federal sources is for compensatory education of children from low-income and culturally deprived circumstances. Other funds have been appropriated for education of handicapped children, for vocational education, and for other categorical purposes. The federal government appropriates approximately 8 percent of the total dollars spent in elementary and secondary schools, while 92 percent comes from state and local sources. These nationwide percentages may vary somewhat from one state to another. However, the total influence of the federal government in the field of education is still quite limited. Many observers believe that the federal government should appropriate many times more dollars than is currently being done and that there should be more federal direction in the field of education. Others, however, support the point of view that we should retain local and state control of education and that the federal influence should be kept to a minimum.

Parents should become knowledgeable about the issues of federal aid and federal control of education. Those who want to preserve the right of electing persons close to the community to manage the schools must be diligent. Grass-roots control of education has been justifiably criticized. The biggest problem is parent complacency and lack of involvement in matters that relate to education. The federal government—through its courts and its regulating agencies—is having as much or even a greater impact on education, as in the federal financial assistance program. This is particularly true regarding racial balance, desegregation, and busing to provide compliance with court orders. Federal direction, regulations, and intervention through the federal courts are all shaping educational policy and practice.

DEALING WITH THE SCHOOL BUREAUCRACY

As a parent of school age children you should be actively involved in matters that relate to the governance of education. The system was designed to give you and your neighbors a voice. By being active in the political party of your choice, and by participating aggressively in the PTA organization, you will be able to influence decisions that affect equality of education in your neighborhood and community. More specific information on this subject is provided in Appendix B.

Appendix B
Parents, PTA's, and School Boards

When the founding fathers drafted the Constitution of the United States, it was their intention that parents have a large role in the education of their children. The responsibility for education was delegated to the states. This delegation, however, did not represent a view that education was unimportant in the minds of those leaders who established our form of government; the choice was a deliberate one to delegate responsibility for education in a way that would keep it close to the people. In keeping with this concept, most of the states have delegated to the counties, cities, or local communities the major voice in governing the schools. In almost all of the states, schools are governed at the grass-roots level by local school boards. Most school board members are elected by the people, although there are some states where they are appointed.

PARENT AND TEACHERS' ASSOCIATION

National, state, and local PTA organizations have been formed to provide a means through which parents can participate in public school affairs. Contrary to common belief, parent and teachers' associations have had a profound impact upon American education. The PTA movement, despite its many accomplishments, however, has never realized its *full* potential. This organization is, of course, committed to students. Benefits to school employee groups from efforts of the PTA are only incidental to the larger goal of student advocacy. More than any other educational organization, the PTA has a commitment first and ever to children. PTA has never received the recognition merited for many very significant contributions to American public education. This is largely because of the nature of the PTA organization. It is not a self-serving establishment. There are no reasons to have publicity campaigns and public relations efforts to build the image of PTA or to herald the accomplishments of this organization. To be sure, there are notable instances where PTA organizations have been listless in performance. But this is not the overall record of PTA in the history of American education.

Progress made in many areas of school services in most of the states was originated by PTA action groups. For example, PTA has been largely responsible for the school food service program in the schools. The progress made in providing better health and safety services, curriculum improvements, better counseling services, and many other programs of educational service to children have been initiated by various PTA organizations.

PARENTING AND THE PTA

If your PTA organization is not as dynamic as it should be, perhaps this is a place where you can make a great contribution. From the discussion that follows you should learn more about PTA, how it is organized, and how you might become more deeply involved in helping to advance its worthy purposes.

In most school systems the PTA has a local unit in every school. Officers are elected by member parents and teachers. Committees are appointed to carry out certain programs and functions. Special educational services and school improvement projects are launched each year. In many PTA organizations the school principal serves as a vice-president in the local organization. Usually, an active parent is elected as president. Other officers are selected from persons known to be active and interested in PTA.

In recent years our secondary schools have changed the designation from PTA to PTSA. The S, of course, represents students. More students are becoming participants in PTSA affairs in junior and senior high schools. But more needs to be done to get student involvement in this fine organization. The public schools need to have a larger voice of expression from our older and more mature students. Students need to learn more about active participation in community affairs through organizations such as PTSA. Not only will there be a contribution made to PTSA, but student involvement will enhance the educational endeavors of the school by teaching students how to get results and how to be heard on issues. This will, of course, pay off in the curriculum responsibility of teaching active citizenship duties.

Most school systems have a PTA council organization made up of a group of local PTA units. The council usually meets in the school district headquarters offices. The superintendent of schools and his staff work with the council members in helping to advance PTA on a district-wide basis. The PTA council may be one of several in a large school district or it may be the only council in a small or medium-sized system. The number of councils is usually determined by the size and complexity of the school district.

Most PTA councils have a president, other officers, and an executive board. This group is elected by the local PTA officials to represent local problems and projects on the school district headquarters level. Problems that have their origin or potential for solution at the district headquarters office can be dealt with by the PTA council organization.

In most states the PTA councils have a large voice in state PTA matters. Annual state PTA conventions are held in most of the states. Officers to manage state-level affairs are elected at these conventions by delegates from PTA councils of each school district.

The state PTA organizations are usually very active in working with the state legislature to get laws passed and appropriations made for schools. In some states the PTA is a very influential force in shaping school legislation. In others, the level of activity is such that very little political power is exercised on school matters at the state capital.

In most states, State Departments of Education and State Boards of Education are deeply involved in state-level PTA affairs. State PTA officers meet regularly with the chief state school officer and with other State Department of Education officials.

State PTA officials appear often before State Boards of Education to express views and influence policy and administrative decisions that are made on the state level.

THE POWER AND INFLUENCE OF PTA

In some localities the PTA is a standard joke. Influential people mistakenly make fun of the local PTA as an organization that meets often and does next to nothing. Unfortunately, this criticism is justified in some PTA organizations. But in recent years the state, council, and local PTA units have become increasingly influential in school affairs. Wise and alert school administrators have found the PTA organizations capable of much valuable work. Fortunately, in some instances local school superintendents and school boards have been goaded into action by a dynamic PTA organization that has become concerned about problems and issues needing attention in the school district.

This much can be said about the potential of PTA: This organization is gaining in power. It is potentially much more powerful than it currently is, and many PTA leaders are recognizing this political fact of life. School board members, state senators and representatives, governors, and U.S. Congressmen and Senators are feeling this new political power of PTA groups. Being a grass-roots organization, with a local unit in almost every city, town, and village in the United States, PTA has enormous potential. Politicians and political parties are just now beginning to "discover" PTA.

In past years PTA has tried unsuccessfully to avoid controversy and to be somewhat neutral in issues where sides are taken and political battles are fought. This reluctance to enter controversial fields has been fading recently. PTA still avoids partisan politics, and this is as it should be. But PTA groups have been taking very aggressive positions in matters where student needs and student rights are at issue. Recent success in shaping policy and in getting legislation passed has led to the entry of more PTA organizations into fields of controversy. All of this has helped to build a new image of PTA on the national, state, and local levels. It is true that some PTA groups have been burned a few times by backing the wrong candidate for school boards, legislature, or Congress. But these incidents are few and far between. In most instances the entry of PTA into controversial areas has resulted in positive benefits in advancing the cause of the public school system.

Some politicians have tried to use PTA as a stepping-stone to political power. A few have even succeeded where their records were good and a solid reputation for education was fully justified. More pressure to involve PTA in politics will be in the offing. The PTA, with its grass-roots type of organizational structure, is a natural for political action. Education is a great cause for any political aspirant to champion. The real challenge for PTA in the years ahead will be for its leadership to support those issues and back those candidates that will enhance educational opportunities for students. It will take some wisdom and discretion to do this without getting involved in partisan politics *per se.*

There has been an encouraging trend of a more action-oriented PTA in recent years. More prestigious and dynamic leaders are being elected to PTA positions of responsibility. The PTA has great potential and is showing ever-increasing promise as a powerful influence in school board, county commission, city commission, and state legislative meetings. The new PTA movement is a far cry from what existed even a few years ago.

YOUR ROLE IN PTA

As a parent of school age children you should be actively involved in PTA affairs. If the meetings seem to be dull and irrelevant, raise your voice. If you care about the education of your children, if you want to be able to influence school policy and decision-making at the local, school district, state, and national levels, *get involved* in PTA. If you would like to become a leader in your community in many matters related to education and improvement of conditions for youth, *get involved* in PTA.

Many PTA organizations need better leadership. Many need more members who care and who will contribute time and effort. You will find a source of great satisfaction and fulfillment in becoming an active leader in PTA work. Moreover, PTA will provide a means for you to get better acquainted with your children's teachers and with school administrators. PTA may be the key to some of the educational problems of your children. It may offer you the opportunity you would like to have to serve your neighbors, your community, and your local and state government.

Unfortunately, fathers have not been very active in PTA organizations. It is still unusual to attend a local PTA meeting and find many fathers in the audience. PTA needs more active men as well as women helping to advance the purposes of this fine organization.

Whether PTA reaches its full potential in the years ahead will depend largely upon individual parents. PTA should not be the captive of militant teacher organizations nor of self-serving school administrators. It should speak for youth, for the neighborhood, and for the city, county, and state insofar as education and child opportunities are concerned. This is not to imply that teacher organizations and school administrators are not dedicated to youth and the advancement of education, but rather that the voice of PTA cannot be misinterpreted since it is not made up exclusively of school district employees.

PTA should steer the difficult course between being aggressively involved in issues affecting children and being very carefully aloof from *partisan* politics and from identification with a particular political party. To be powerful on some key issues while remaining aloof from partisanship will take real wisdom and insight on the part of PTA leaders. In this fine art, some toes will be stepped on and some outcries of rage will be heard. But PTA must become more aggressive and more demanding on issues where children will either benefit or be hurt.

Individual parents should use PTA as a means of serving children and of carrying out part of the civic duties inherent in citizenship. PTA needs more active prestigious people who are recognized leaders in the community. This wholesome trend of involvement of community leaders in PTA is gratifying to all who see the great potential of this organization. PTA needs more of the very busy and influential leaders than it is now getting. This is a great challenge for PTA leaders in the years ahead.

There are very few higher callings in life than that which leads to building a better future for our youth. Few organizations provide the opportunity for leadership and service that PTA affords. You should reexamine your role and commitment to your children and to your children's friends. In this examination you will hopefully find an opportunity to serve in a much more influential and meaningful way the needs of youth through enhancing the great cause of public school education through the Parent Teachers' Association.

WORKING WITH LOCAL SCHOOL BOARD MEMBERS

In Appendix A some discussion was offered concerning the role of school board members. The legal structure of local school boards and their relationships to state and national government were covered. But more needs to be said about the local school board member's role in helping to improve educational opportunity at home as well as at school. Here we will discuss further the local school board member and his or her relationship to the neighborhood school and to education as it has impact upon the children in your home.

Keep in mind that a member of a school board must function as part of the total board. The board member must abide by the rules and regulations of the total board of education. Board members must not interfere in the operations of your neighborhood school by giving the principal, teachers, or other school employees instructions. This is the duty of the superintendent of schools. It is important for you to keep this fact clearly in mind as you call your school board member and ask him or her to do things that need to get done in the local school. A board member can be responsive to your call, but must go through the proper channels in taking care of your concern. Principals and other school employees should receive their instructions from the superintendent of schools and not from board members. Therefore, your local school board member will not be able to interfere directly in matters that are of concern to you. But a board member who plays his or her role effectively will be able to discuss the problem through proper channels and get the desired results.

Most school employees are very responsive to members of boards of education. Board members have broad powers when they sit in official board meetings. Therefore, the impression should not be given that your problems will not receive attention if you call your local school board member. On the contrary, he or she can be very influential in calling attention of the proper authorities to urgent matters.

But the board member has a responsibility to sit with other board members to shape school policy and to make decisions for the entire school district. Board members act officially when the board of education is in official session. Outside of board meetings the school board member must be careful not to commit the entire board to a position. Each board member must respect the rights of other members of the board. This does not mean that the board member should not explain and defend school policy. However, he or she must use the official channels of the school district to influence the policy-making and administration of the school system. If you keep this situation in mind, you will be more effective in your discussions with your local school board member as you strive to persuade your board member to accept your point of view.

Board members have a responsibility to listen to complaints and suggestions. You should feel free to call your board member on matters of concern to you, but keep in mind the relationship of the board member to the school, to the other school board members, and to the superintendent of schools. If your board member does not give an immediate opinion or answer your question fully, it is likely that he or she will want to get further information and confer with others before pushing for some action.

School board members either serve without pay or serve under a token payment of very little significance. Many hours are demanded of members of boards of education. They are often called at home by parents, staff members, and employees. They have regular responsibilities of earning a living in addition to the school board service that is rendered. Parents should be aware of these demands upon local school board members and should be considerate of added time demands placed upon them.

Your local school board member represents government at the grass-roots level. There are very few governmental units operated as close to the communities and neighborhoods as are local school districts. The school board helps to set school policies on such matters as employment and working conditions of staff, local property tax levies and budgets, locating sites for construction of future schools, school bus routes and transportation policy, educational standards and regulations. Every month your local school board member is involved in decision-making that will touch your home and have an impact upon educational conditions for your children.

Some of these decisions are very difficult to make. Some parents expect services such as door-to-door school bus service. This is, of course, a demand that is hard to meet. The local school board must set regulations concerning transportation service. What is a reasonable distance for children to walk to school? Wherever boundary is set for transportation service, the probabilities are high that some school patrons will be disappointed because they live right next to the cutoff point. The same applies to such issues as birth date deadlines when children will be admitted to school for kindergarten or first grade. No matter where this date is set, some children will be within a few days of reaching the deadline. But if these deadlines are not set and certain rules enforced, a chaotic condition will develop. Attendance rules, student discipline, placement of teachers and employment of school principals, adoption of textbooks, and numerous other decisions made by the board of education may be highly controversial. There are times when board members must sit at the decision-making table and vote on an issue that is unpopular with some neighbors. The challenge of school board membership is very demanding. Parents should strive to see the issues in perspective and to realize that some decisions may have to be made that are not favorable to particular sectors. These decisions usually generate strong feelings that place board members in the center of controversy. But someone must make these decisions. It is better that they be made on a level that is most sensitive to the desires of the greatest majority of the people. Local control of public schools is fundamental to the need of keeping education responsive to the wishes of parents. It is better to have decisions made by neighbors and fellow citizens answerable to the parents and taxpayers in the community. The decentralized system is a great tradition and a fundamental strength of American public education. Parents should remember to express their thanks for the conscientious men and women who render the great civic service of serving on a school board.

You should follow closely the decisions of your local board of education. The record of each board member should be well known to you when you vote. Too many parents pay little attention to the records of these important officials who make such far-reaching decisions. You can help to keep dedicated, enlightened, and conscientious men and women serving on the local school board.

HOW TO GET OUTSTANDING SCHOOL BOARD MEMBERS ELECTED

The best school board members are usually the most successful people. They are usually very busy and involved in many activities in the community. Most outstanding board members serve on school boards because of the appeal of performing a civic duty. You should strive to help improve your school system by encouraging your outstanding community leaders to run for the school board.

Be sure to know when school board filing deadlines expire for candidates. This information can usually be obtained by calling the school district office or by calling the county clerk at the county courthouse. Learn about filing procedures, and get the names of your candidates filed early.

Most school board elections are nonpartisan. You ordinarily will not need to work through the political party machinery in getting support for your candidate. It is useful, of course, to gain support from all sources, and if political leaders can be persuaded to lend support to your candidate it will be all the better.

You should not only select and persuade capable and dedicated leaders to run for election, but you should also choose candidates that will be able to meet the public, and will make a good public impression.

Your candidate for the school board should have ample opportunity to become known to air his or her views on education. An organization of active parents covering the area to be represented by your school board candidate may want to assist with telephone calls and printing and mailing literature.

Appendix C
Recommended Reading

Following is a list of references that I believe will be of the most value to parents of preschool and school age children. This is not a complete or exhaustive list. There are obviously many other useful writings. But if you are interested in doing some further study to enhance your understanding of home-based learning and about child growth and development, these books will be of particular value to you.

Bell, Terrel H. *Your Child's Intellect.* Salt Lake City: Olympus Publishing Company, 1972.
>A parents' guide to home-based preschool education. Has section at the end of each chapter on practical use of common materials in the home that can be used as teaching aids.

Briggs, Dorothy C. *Your Child's Self-Esteem.* New York: Doubleday, 1970.

This is an excellent source book for parents who have children with self-image problems and for children who lack self-confidence.

Button, Alan DeWitt, *The Authentic Child.* New York: Random House, 1969.
Advocates spontaneous and open relationships between parent and child. Considerable emphasis is given to being human, natural, and totally open and candid with children. An excellent source for parents seeking to establish better rapport with their children.

Cohen, Dorothy M. *The Learning Child: Guidelines for Parents and Teachers.* New York: Random House, 1972.
This book places great emphasis on personal integrity and moral development. The importance of the home in nurturing child growth and learning is discussed in considerable detail.

Evans, Thomas W. *The School in the Home.* New York: Harper and Row, 1973.
This book claims that the intelligence of the child can be increased if the parent leads the growth of vocabulary in the early years. A great amount of emphasis is given to parental responsibility.

Gesell, Arnold. *The First Five Years of Life: A Guide to the Study of the Preschool Child.* New York: Harper, 1940.
Although this is obviously not a work of recent vintage, it is still a classic on early childhood. It is easy reading and provides an excellent background to early child development.

Ginott, Haim C. *Between Parent and Child.* New York: Macmillan Company, 1965.
This book is a rich source of information about conversation with children. Many ideas on how to deal with the emotional problems of children are described in clear, easy to understand language.

Ginott, Haim C. *Between Parent and Teenager.* New York: Macmillan Company, 1969.

The reader will learn about the problems of expressing too much criticism and of lecturing to teenagers. Parents are advised about how to handle problems of drinking, drugs, sex, dating, and dress. A good source book for parents of teenagers.

Gordon, Thomas. *Parent Effectiveness Training.* (paperback). New York: New American Library, 1975.

This widely read source teaches parents how to interact with children of all ages. It is full of practical illustrations and true-to-life episodes that help the reader to grasp the methodology advocated by the author. An unusually practical book based on years of study and experience.

Hunt, J. McVicker. *Intelligence and Experience.* New York: The Ronald Press Company, 1961.

Treats the role of experience in developing intelligence. The book is exceptionally well written. It will help the reader to understand the importance of experiences in the home in helping to build a more powerful intellect.

Larrick, Nancy. *A Parent's Guide to Children's Reading.* New York: Doubleday, 1969.

This is without doubt a very useful book for parents interested in stimulating children to read. It is full of information about children's books and it has many helpful and practical ideas.

Spock, Benjamin. *The Common Sense Book of Baby and Child Care.* New York: Duell, Sloan and Pearce, 1945.

This old classic is still valuable reading for parents.

White, Burton L. *The First Three Years of Life.* Englewood Cliffs, N.J.: Prentice-Hall, 1975.

This book represents, in the author's opinion, the best source of practical information available concerning the early years of life. Actively concerned parents and expectant parents will find this excellent book to be a treasure house of knowledge.

INDEX

Achievement tests, 108-15
    administration of, 111
    comparison of schools through scores on, 114
    grade-placement norm of, 109-10
    improvement in taking, 111-13
    influence of school and home on, 114-15
    item analysis of, 110
    limitations of, 113
    percentile norms of, 110
Action-oriented guidelines, 4-5
Adaptation and adjustment to school, 62-63
AFL-CIO, 173
Ambition, 56-58
American Federation of Teachers, 173
Arts curriculum
    in home, 53-54
    in school, 92-94
Authentic Child, The (Button), 187

Bell, Terrel H., 186
Between Parent and Child (Ginott), 187
Between Parent and Teenager (Ginott), 127n, 187-88
Board of education, local, 166-69
Briggs, Dorothy C., 186
Bureaucracy, school system, 163-75
Button, Alan DeWitt, 187

Calls from school, 60-62
Careers, 131-32
    curriculum and, 79-80, 88-91
    school counseling and, 137-38
Character, 56-58
Child-perceived disasters, 30-31
Child self-concept, parent responsibility for, 31-33
Cohen, Dorothy M., 187
Common Sense Book of Baby and Child Care, The (Spock), 188
Community, family orientation toward, 12
Compassion, 15
Competence, social, 55-56
Competitive relationships, 29-30
Content of conversations, 7-8
Conversation
    clear and spontaneous, 12
    content of, 7-8
    with older children and youth, 127-29
    as teaching, 43
Corrective instruction, 80-81

Counseling
    group, 135
    at home, 123-32
    home room, 136
    at school, 123-24, 132-38
Counselors, school, 132-33
Courts, 166
Crisis situations, 130-31
Criticism, nondefensiveness to, 14
Cultural bias of tests, 102
Curriculum, 73-99
    arts and humanities in, 92-94
    career decisions and planning of, 79-80, 88-91
    depth emphasis and, 77-79
    extracurricular activities and, 94-99
    health and physical education in, 91-92
    home based, 35-58
    language arts in, 82-84
    limitless educational opportunity in, 76-77
    mathematics in, 84-85
    overview of, 74
    parent counseling and, 74-76, 81-82
    remedial and correction instruction in, 80-81
    science in, 86-87
    social studies in, 85-86

Department of education, state, 165-66
Differences of opinion, 13
Disasters, child-perceived, 30-31
Discipline, 7
Discouragement, failure in school and, 151
Disposition, stable, 14
Distortion in conversation, 12-13
Drive, 56-58

Early childhood, intelligence and, 119
Education
    financing of, 171-72
    high potential for, 11-14
    objectives and purposes of, 45-48
    technical, 131-32
Education associations, 172-74
Election to local school boards, 184-85
Essay tests, 103-4
Evans, Thomas W., 22n, 49n, 187
Examinations, 101-21
    achievement, 108-15
    advice to parents on, 119-21
    essay, 103-4

INDEX

Examinations, *continued*
   intelligence or IQ, 115-19
   multiple-choice, 104-5
   possible cultural bias of, 104-5
   recall-type, 105-6
   standardized, 102-3, 108-15
   teacher follow-up on, 106-8
   teacher-made, 102-8
   true-false, 105

Failure in school, 139-52
   assessing facts on, 146
   avoiding discouragement in face of, 151
   course of action on, 147-48
   getting facts on, 140-44
   goals and recognition, 150-51
   physical well-being and, 150
   positive outlook and, 150
   potential of home and, 146-47
   professional help and, 151-52
   removing obstacles at home and, 148-50
   school counselor and, 145-46
   self-image and, 144
   teacher and, 144-45, 148
Family life, learning and, 1-20
Father, 13
Feelings of children, 7
Financing of public schools, 171-72
First Five Years of Life: A Guide to the Study of the Preschool Child (Gesell), 187
First Three Years of Life, The (White), 188
Federal government, 174-75
Frequency of conversations, 7-8
Friends, 16
Frugality, 16
Frustration, 15

Genuine conversations, 7
Gesell, Arnold, 187
Ginott, Haim C., 127*n*, 187-88
Gordon, Thomas, 5*n*, 188
Governor, local school and, 164-65
Grade-placement norms, 109-10
Group counseling, 135
Guidance and counseling
   at home, 123-32
   at school, 123-24, 132-38

Health curriculum
   in home, 55
   in school, 91-92
Healthy personality, 14-17
Home
   failure in school and, 146-50
   influence on achievement of, 114-15
   influence on personality of, 17-19
Home based curriculum, 35-58
   health and physical activity in, 55
   incidental teaching and, 36-45
   language and, 49-50
   mathematics and, 50-51
   music, art and literature in, 53-55
   school curriculum and, 44

Home curriculum, *continued*
   scientific method and, 51-52
   social competence in, 55-56
   social sciences and, 52-53
Home counseling, 123-32
   school curriculum and, 74-76, 81-82
   of teenagers, 127-32
Home room counseling activities, 136
Humane living, principles of, 52-53
Humanities curriculum, 92-94
Humor, sense of, 15
Hunt, J. McVicker, 23*n*, 188

Ideals, nurturing, 131
Incidental teaching method, 35-58
Independence, 13
Individualized counseling, school, 136-37
Inner-directedness, 16
Inner drive, 21
Instruction, remedial, 80-81
Intelligence and Experience (Hunt), 23*n*, 188
Intelligence tests, 115-19
Interest, demonstration of, 8-9
Interpersonal relationships with children, 159
IQ tests, 115-19
Item analysis of achievement tests, 110

Language arts curriculum
   in home, 49-50
   in school, 82-84
Larrick, Nancy, 188
Learning, family life and, 1-20
Learning Child: Guidelines for Parents and Teachers, The (Cohen), 187
Legislature, state, 164
Listening to children, 5-8
Literature in home, 53-54
Local schools, *see* Schools
Local school boards, 166-69, 182-85
Love, 28-29

Mathematics curriculum
   in home, 50-51
   in school, 84-85
Mother, 13
Motivation
   guidelines on, 22-27
   review and evaluation of climate for, 27-28
   self image and, 21-33
Multiple-choice test, 104-5
Music, 53-54

National Education Association, 172-73
Neighborhood, family orientation toward, 12
Nondefensiveness to criticism, 14

Parent Effectiveness Training (Gordon), 5*n*, 188
Parent, Teacher, Students' Association (PTSA), 178
Parent Teachers' Association (PTA), 176-81

INDEX

Parent volunteers in school, 69
Parenting, PTA and, 177-79
Parent's Guide to Children's Reading, A (Larrick), 188
Parents, single, 19-20
Percentile norms, 110
Permanent record folder, 133-35
Personality
    healthy, 14-17
    influence of home on, 17-19
Physical activity in home, 55
Physical education curriculum, 91-92
Physical well-being, failure in school and, 150
Positive attitudes, 1-20
    failure in school and, 150
    in self-image, 28-30
Potential for education, 11-14
Principal, responsibilities of, 67-69
Problem teachers, 9-11
Professional help, failure in school and, 151-52
PTA (Parent Teachers' Association), 176-81
Public schools, *see* School
Punishment, 27

Questioning, skill of, 44-45

Realism about capacities, 14
Recall-type tests, 105-6
Records, school, 133-35
Remedial instruction, 80-81
Report cards, 60-62
    See also Failure

School, 59-71
    adaptation and adjustment to, 62-63
    compared through achievement test results, 114
    day, 59-60
    failure in, 139-52
    financing of, 171-72
    influence on achievement of, 114-15
    parent volunteers in, 69
    principal and, 67-69
    responding to reports and calls from, 60-62
    school system bureaucracy and, 69-71, 163-75
    teachers and, 63-67
    working with, 8-9
School board, local, 166-69, 182-85
    election of outstanding members to, 184-85
    working with, 182-84
    See also School system
School counseling, 123-24, 132-38
School counselors, 132-33
    failure in school and, 145-46
School day, 59-60
School in the Home, The (Evans), 22n, 49n, 187
School records, 133-35

School system, local school and, 69-71
    See also School board, local
Science curriculum, 86-87
Scientific method, 51-52
Self-concept, 31-33
Self-discipline, 15
Self-governing children, 12
Self-image
    failure in school and, 144
    motivation and, 21-33
    positive, 28-30
Sense of humor, 15
Sex matters, parental counsel on, 129-30
Single parents, 19-20
Skill training, 131-32
Social competence, 55-56
Social studies curriculum
    in home, 52-53
    in school, 85-86
Spock, Benjamin, 188
Stable disposition, 14
Standardized testing, 102-3, 108-19
    achievement, 108-15
    intelligence or IQ, 115-19
State department of education, 165-66
State legislature, 164
Superintendent of schools, 169-70

Teachers
    failure in school and, 144-45, 148
    getting to know, 63-66
    problem, 9-11
    teaching loads and, 66-67
    tests made by, 102-8
Teachers' unions, 172-74
Teaching loads, 66-67
Teaching method, incidental, 35-58
Technical education, 131-32
Teenagers, home counseling of, 127-32
Tests, 101-21
    achievement, 108-15
    advice to parents on, 119-21
    essay, 103-4
    intelligence or IQ, 115-19
    multiple-choice, 104-5
    possible cultural bias of, 102
    recall-type, 105-6
    standardized, 102-3, 108-19
    teacher follow-up on result of, 106-8
    teacher-made, 102-8
    true-false, 105
Training, skill, 131-32
True-false tests, 105

Unions, teachers, 172-74

Vocational education, 88-91
Volunteers, parent, 69

White, Burton L., 188
Will, 56-58

Your Child's Intellect (Bell), 186
Your Child's Self-Esteem (Bell), 186

191